EDIFYING
THE
BODY
OF
CHRIST

MINISTER **BRENDA JOHNSON**

authorHOUSE®

AuthorHouse™
1663 Liberty Drive
Bloomington, IN 47403
www.authorhouse.com
Phone: 1 (800) 839-8640

Published by AuthorHouse   10/14/2019

ISBN: 978-1-7283-2890-4 (sc)
ISBN: 978-1-7283-2889-8 (e)

Contents

1

REVERENCE IN THE SANCTUARY

THE HOUSE OF GOD

The house of God—In the ancient tabernacle, which was God's house, the symbol of the Divine Majesty dwelt as the Arc of the Covenant. Today, the Christian Church is God's house, and every believer is a habitation of God through the Spirit because the Spirit of God dwells in every believer. We must understand when we come to church that we are coming to God's House, where His presence is. It is where the things of God are kept, where the people of God assemble. We should reverence His house and His things and handle them with care. We must not take them lightly. Respect the physical building, the furnishings, including the alter, the podium, the communion table and the equipment. The same is true even for the floors and carpeting. The entire facility, bathrooms and fellowship areas should be respected for the set apart use that they are designated for.

1 Timothy 3:15 AMP

"… that you may know how people ought to conduct themselves in the household of God, which is the church of the living God, the pillar and stay (the prop and support) of the Truth."

THE SANCTITY OF THE SANCTUARY

The church of God is such a special fellowship, the very household of the Lord, that people must conduct themselves in it correctly. **Jesus said** My house shall be called a house of prayer.

This should be for all who enter. They should know they are entering a house of prayer. One should see prayer, feel prayer and do prayer. When one enters, the house should be saturated with such a spirit of prayer that they want to immediately fall to their knees and begin to pray. Everyone who enters God's house may not already be saved, but that doesn't keep them from feeling that spirit of prayer and worship that should exude from every corner, especially from the sanctuary.

What is a sanctuary? It is a sacred or holy place. It is a place particularly designated or consecrated for holy acts, (i.e. prayer, praise, worship, baptism, communion, installation, ordination etc.).

Because it is set apart for holy worship, there should be no inappropriate behavior that would distract (take one's focus) or detract (quench the Spirit) from attaining that purpose. God's presence abides strong in this holy place. If we come in for any other reason than to give worship to God, we are out of order.

GOING TO CHURCH

Psalm 122:1 KJV –"I was glad when they said unto me, let us go into the house of the LORD."

People come to church for different reasons. They come with different attitudes and expectations.

- Some come to greet their friends and fellowship with them
- Some come out of habit
- Some come to appease their conscience
- Some actually come to be seen or heard
- Some come to hear the word preached or taught
- To gain knowledge and understanding
- Many people come to enjoy the music, the singing and the dancing
- Some come to watch others get blessed (to spectate)
- Some come with negative spirits to hinder the move of God
- Some come to discourage praise and worship
- To discourage the preacher
- To cause division with a critical look or critical word

We are God's people whom He made to worship Him. Any other spirit is a disappointment to Him. **The word** says that He is looking for worshippers.

But the hour cometh, and now is, when the true worshippers shall worship the Father in spirit and in truth: for the Father seeketh such to worship him.

So, leave all the negative reasons and spirits outside.

There is preparation to be made before we go to church, so as to ensure our highest focus on God and His Word. The negative thoughts from the above list should be headed off and cast down and brought into the obedience of Christ. We should begin prayer for one another even before we get to church, so that we come in a spirit of love. To the extent that we can, we should do our physical preparation the day before, so that on that morning, we are not running around flustered and exhausted before we even get to church. We should go to bed on time and get up on time. Play your favorite worship or praise music on the way and let your spirit join in with it. These little hints will help us to arrive at church with the right spirit, rested, blessed and ready for God's word.

3

HERE I AM LORD

When we enter, we can tell God**, HERE I AM LORD,**

- ➢ I have come Lord out from my home, over the roads, in spite of my circumstances and conditions, I've made my way here.
- ➢ I have come to your house to meet with you, to present my body as a living Sacrifice.
- ➢ Lord, I have come here to be in your presence.
- ➢ Lord I humbly bow before You and reverence Your great name.
- ➢ There is none like You, and I honor You.
- ➢ I'm here for You and You only.
- ➢ My focus is on You. Nothing and no one else gets any of this time that I have dedicated to You.
- ➢ I will not be distracted by people.
- ➢ Lord, here I am to worship You and to tell You --- You are my God, and I love You.

Yes, some come joyfully. Some come dragging, barely making it. Yet all arrive expecting something---to be saved, healed, delivered and set free from whatever their bondage is. But all owe God reverence and thank you just for even being able to get to church. The least we can give Him is sincere worship and our full attention. So, "enter into His gates with Thanksgiving and into His courts with praise. Be thankful unto Him and bless His name". **(Ps 100:4 KJV)**

2

SERVE GOD-NOT SELF

God wants us to serve Him and not put ourselves, anyone or anything else before Him. God demanded of Moses that His people be released to serve Him. We have to make a decision to serve God, to live our lives to please Him first. Although God is loving and merciful, He is also a jealous God, and there will be consequences for not giving Him His due place of eminence in our lives. Serving God is the ultimate pleasure and ultimate satisfaction because it fulfills the purpose for which we were created. It provides the only thing that is designed to fill the void we all carry.

BEWARE OF COVETOUSNESS

The Bible tells us to take heed about living our lives to accumulate wealth and things.

Luke 12:15 KJV- "And he said unto them, Take heed, and beware of covetousness: for a man's life consisteth not in the abundance of the things which he possesseth."

If we are chasing money and fame, the Bible warns us that our life does not lie in material things. You could spend your time on earth chasing and gathering material things and miss the opportunity to live the abundant life that God came to provide.

LAWLESS LIVING

It is possible to over-indulge ourselves to an extent that it becomes out of control. One of the fruit of the Spirit is temperance, or self-control, but when our carnal nature is in control (our flesh), we will deny it nothing, and our only goal is to do whatever will please it.

If you spend your life on carnal pleasures such as food, drink, unrestrained living, you won't find fulfillment. You can't eat enough, drink enough, have enough sex, get high enough or get enough degrees to fill the real void in your life. That void points us to our need to serve God.

Only the one who made us knows what it will take to fill our need in such a way that leaves us wanting nothing.

THOU FOOL

Luke 12:20 KJV– "But God said unto him, Thou fool, this night thy soul shall be required of thee: then whose shall those things be, which thou hast provided?"

I used to think about how good it must be to be retired with good health and sufficient finances. I thought that it should bring the ultimate happiness to be able to spend all your time doing only what pleases you. Then I realized it's like being able to drive only one car at a time although you may own many. There is only so much pleasure one can enjoy before it ends. Material and natural pleasures are temporary and still leave you with a void that is unfilled. "…For the things that are seen are temporal, but the things that are not seen are eternal." (**2Cor 4:18 KJV**) We need to value heavenly things, things that are important to God... how we are living our lives to serve Him.

ONLY WHAT YOU DO FOR CHRIST WILL LAST

Matt. 6:19-20 KJV– "Lay not up for yourselves treasures upon earth, where moth and rust doth corrupt, and where thieves break through and steal:

But lay up for yourselves treasures in heaven, where neither moth nor rust doth corrupt, and where thieves do not break through nor steal."

3

THE SOVEREIGNTY OF GOD

The Sovereignty of God is His indisputable supreme authority and power over this universe, including everything and everybody in it. That it is indisputable is declared in **Matt 28:18 KJV** where Jesus says, "all power is given unto me in heaven and in earth". No one can challenge or stand up against His power and authority.

He is God in heaven and rules over all the kingdoms of the heathen, and none can withstand Him. In other words, He rules over the saved and the unsaved.

That He is supreme (above and before all things) is seen in **Col. 1:16 KJV** which says "by Him were all things created in heaven and in earth, visible and invisible... All things were created by Him and for Him" (for His glory).

A COMFORTING THOUGHT

Isn't it comforting to know that there is no other power that can over-rule God? Ultimately, the buck stops with His Word. **Num. 23:19 KJV "**... hath (God) spoken, and shall He not make it good?**"** Yes, if God said so, He will bring it to pass.

God is sovereign over our lives even when we don't choose to obey Him. His Word tells us what the consequences will be for disobedience. He is God whether we cooperate or not. We will just have to eat the fruit of our choices. God is glorified and pleased when we choose to obey Him. That is why He has given us free will. God's sovereignty will carry out His will with or without any individual. "Thy Kingdom come. Thy will be done in earth as it is in heaven". (**Matt. 6:10 KJV**)

FOLLOW GOD'S AGENDA

God is master and maker of the universe. Nothing happens unless He allows it. We can have visions and agendas toward reaching them, but we must seek direction from God for reaching any goals that we set for ourselves. We want to set goals that are in agreement with God's plan for us. If we do this, we'll know that we will achieve the exceeding abundant success that God intends for us. God's plans for us are for our good and not evil, so that He will give us an expected end (the end that He expects for us).

A SAFETY NET

God's sovereignty is the "safety net" for us. Because He is master and in control, He's working out all things for our good according to His purpose.

What is His purpose? His purpose is always for our welfare and for His glory. He loves us with an everlasting love. Therefore, we can rest in the fact that He is sovereign and in charge. Whatever the circumstances, whatever we go through, we can know that it's working ultimately for our good, in the long run.

THE SHORT AND LONG OF IT

God knows and sees the short-run and the long-run. Our times are in His hands.

"To everything there is a **season**, and a **time** to every purpose under the heaven." (**Ecc. 3:1 KJV**) We have to be willing to wait on the Lord.

He is the first and the last, and the beginning and the end. From everlasting to everlasting, He is God. Because of His sovereignty, there is nothing on this earth that we need to fear, as long as our faith and trust is in Him. He will be there for us. He is "a very present help in trouble." (**Ps. 46 :1 KJV**)

NONE LIKE HIM

"There is none like God. He has scooped up the ocean in his two hands. He has measured the sky between his thumb and little finger. Who could ever have told GOD what to do or taught Him His business?" (**Is.40:12-14 MSG**) No one.

He will never leave nor forsake us. There is no situation that is too hard for Him to resolve. He is on our side, so who can defeat us?

"God sits high above the round ball of earth". (**Is 40:22 MSG**) There is no other God beside Him and no other Savior. None can compare to Him. None can measure up to Him. "The Lord He is God" (**Deut.4:39 KJV**)

4

A READY SPIRIT

A DESIRE TO BE USED

How many times have we said that we want God to use us? Have we asked Him? When we are asking to be used by God, what are we saying? Do we say that it is our desire and that we are available? The question is are we <u>ready?</u> It is true that God will cause us to do some things to accomplish His purposes, but before He can really do that, He must check out our spirit to see if it is in a usable or ready condition. Yes, there is an evaluation that God must do and a preparation that we must make. If God judges our spirit today, will it be found ready or will it be found wanting?

SPIRITS THAT HINDER

What needs to happen in our spirits to make them ready for God to use? God is not able to use a spirit that is full of demonic attitudes. These things oppose and hinder any purpose of God being accomplished. When we allow demonic spirits to infiltrate our hearts and influence our behavior, we are of no use to God. We render our availability null and void. Spirits such as pride, stubbornness, rebellion and disobedience are demonic and are enemies to God's plans. Included in this list are lying spirits, judgmental spirits, prideful spirits, and spirits of lust. It may be that God may allow us to go through some things that will bring us deliverance in some of these areas.

CHANGING OUR MINDS

Some spirits or attitudes are under our own power to simply "quit", cease to continue. When we can identify attitudes within ourselves that are not pleasing to God, we can ask for forgiveness and repent of them.

To repent means that we "change" our attitude or way of thinking regarding that behavior. When our thinking changes, then our behavior will automatically change. Every action or behavior begins with a thought.

CHARACTERISTICS OF A READY SPIRIT

Even when we have ceased to operate in certain negative attitudes (spirits), we have to be very careful to protect our minds from wandering back in those wrong directions again. Once we are freed from something, we want to remain free and not get tangled back up or drawn back into it in any way.

Pro.4:23 KJV says to "...keep (guard) your heart with all diligence...for out of it are the issues of life". How do we guard our hearts? Although our hearts or spirits are not physical, ideas enter our hearts through physical gateways which are our senses: our eyes, ears, noses, touch and taste. Without these entry ways, our natural bodies do not perceive (experience) the natural world.

Likewise, the **ERV** translation of that verse says that ..." your thoughts control your life." We are to protect our hearts from any thoughts that are contrary to God's word. We can guard our hearts by being selective as to who or what we listen to, where and what we spend our time on, and who or what we look at. We should delight ourselves in the Word of God. We should read it, study it, and meditate on it day and night.

We are to develop and add to ourselves characteristics of virtue, knowledge, temperance, patience, godliness, kindness, love and all the fruit of the Spirit.

We have got to be willing, committed and humble. We must be seeking Him in worship, listening to Him, studying, fasting and praying.

Do you want to be used? Then be willing to put God and His purposes first in your life above all else.

5

PERFECTING THE SAINTS

GOD'S PLAN

It is God's plan that we, as saints, (or believers) submit to a continuing process of growth toward the likeness of Christ. This on-going process of growth toward this goal is the "<u>perfecting</u>" spoken about in the Bible. We know this is Christ's plan because He made provisions for this process to happen. He gave the saints, the body of Christ, persons, as special gifts, whose job it is to bring about this process in our lives. He knew that we could not perfect ourselves. We needed help from outside of ourselves in order for change within ourselves to take place. So, God put His plan in motion so that His intention may be carried out.

THE IMAGE OF GOD

Because we are human beings, God knows that this process of being perfected must continue until we receive our glorified bodies when He comes back for us.

However, until then, we must submit to our perfecting, changing our character from glory to glory as we behold the image of God in His Word.

The image of God is the revelation of God that is seen in His Word. As we will hear his Word and study His Word, we will gain a better understanding of what He looks like (spiritually) and what He does. Only with this understanding will we begin to have a clearer image of Him. We begin to see Him better. Then we can begin to conform to His image.

CHANGING WAYS

Now when His Word is taught to us and preached to us, it is for us to choose to obey. As we obey, we come into agreement with what He says about how we should think and how we should act. So we then begin to change our ways to His ways and our thoughts to His thoughts. **Isaiah 55:8 KJV,** "For my thoughts are not your thoughts, neither are your ways my ways, saith the Lord". We begin to change in our character. Our character begins to reflect (like a mirror) Christ's character. This process of continuous change is repeated again and again as it applies to every aspect of our character that needs changing. As our thoughts change, who we are begins to change. **Pro. 23:7 KJV** says that "as (a man) thinketh in his heart, so is he".

FOR OUR EQUIPPING

God has provided us with persons with special gifts to perfect us: apostles, prophets, evangelists, Pastors and teachers. He also has given and pronounced specific blessings upon us to help toward this purpose. First, of all He provided His written Word that will fully equip us and thoroughly furnish us with His knowledge and instructions. We can learn everything about God by simply reading and studying His Word. In His Word He has made it plain what His expectations of us are. We have no excuse for ignorance when He has provided His Word as our resource.

The Bible, in James 1:4, tells us that if we are patient and steadfast, we will become <u>fully developed</u>, lacking <u>nothing</u>. This is telling us to continue in the perfecting process and stay focused expecting God to do the work in us that is needed.

It also says that He has bestowed upon us all things that are required for life and godly living. In addition, He has given us great and precious promises that will enable us to take part in His divine nature (or character) through <u>personal knowledge of Him.</u> This tells us that as we experience God through obedience to His Word and spending personal time with Him, we will come to know Him and will be able to use this knowledge in order to live a godly life.

It is God who made us and not we ourselves. He knows that by nature, our hearts are wicked. He wills for us to return to the perfect state with which He first created Adam and Eve. They were like Him, innocent and without sin. As He works His plan to move us toward this state, our lives can begin <u>to represent Him,</u> and He will be glorified.

6

THE IMPORTANCE
OF VISION

WITHOUT A VISION

"Where there is no vision, the people perish". (**Pro. 29:18 KJV**) "Where there is no <u>redemptive revelation of God...</u>, the people perish" "Where there is no understanding of the Word of the Lord, the people do whatever they want to". They run wild.

Perish means that they are exposed, uncovered, refuse (or garbage) to be discarded or destroyed. Revelation means a vision of or understanding of a message made clear. Redemptive is that which saves from destruction or redeems or buys back by a price paid. Receiving <u>a clear understanding</u> of how God paid the price for our souls saves us from destruction.

A MESSAGE FROM GOD

When God gives us vision, He is revealing to us a clear understanding of what He wants to communicate to us. This vision is important because it is a message from God. It is meant to guide us and inspire us until that vision is manifested. With the vision before us, we can move in the will of God and avoid directions and actions that would rob us of our time, strength and resources.

We can avoid pitfalls and dangerous detours. When we are pursuing the vision God has given, God will provide whatever we need to complete it.

HITTING THE TARGET

The vision is the goal at the end of a path that we must follow as we depend on God to show us the way. However, the goal is not just a target we're trying to hit. The goal is a means to accomplish a determined purpose, ultimately for God's glory. The determined purpose is what will result from the target being hit. How many lives will be affected for the glory of God? How many people can we share a redemptive revelation of God with? With vision of God and vision from God, we can work to increase the Kingdom of God and His rule here on earth.

VISION OF GOD

We need a right vision of God in order to receive salvation. We need to see Him as Jesus Christ, the Son of the Living God. Then we can believe in His death, burial and resurrection and can accept that He died on the cross for our sins because "God so loved the world that He gave His only begotten Son that whosoever believeth in Him should not perish (should not be destroyed), but have everlasting life." (**John 3:16 KJV**). Then we can believe that He now sits in heaven on the right hand of the Father ever-living to make intercession for us.

VISION FROM GOD

God gives us messages and directives sometimes through visions. Often, these are the times when inventive ideas are born. Through visions, God can give us an entire plan or blueprint of a project He wants us to complete, including the method of how to complete it.

God also gives us vision or revelation through His Word. Through His Word, He directs us how to live our lives. When we read, study and pray, God can make the words of scripture on the page come very much alive in our hearts so that we are able to apply the wisdom of it to our lives.

7

FEAR THOU NOT

DO NOT FEAR

At least thirty times in the Bible, God tells us not to be afraid because He has the situation under His control. He reminds us of who He is and that He will always cause us to emerge from whatever situation in triumph and victory. He promises us that He will never fail us nor leave us helpless without His support. In short, He is always with us. He is <u>Jehovah Shamah</u>, the Lord is there. "God is our refuge and strength, a very present help in trouble, therefore we will not fear…" (**Ps. 46:1-2 KJV**).

GOD'S GOT YOU

God tells us in (**Is. 41:10 KJV**), "Fear thou not; for I am with thee: be not dismayed; for I am thy God: I will strengthen thee; yea, I will help thee; yea I will uphold thee with the right hand of my righteousness." He is telling us that He's got us. Not only does He have our back, but our front and sides also. The enemy cannot defeat us, because we are in God's hand. He is supporting us and defending us with His power.

NOTHING TO FEAR

The enemy will try to intimidate us and make us think that his power can do us harm. However, if we believe that our God is all-powerful and watches over us to protect us, we will not accept any of the enemy's threats. He will use threats against our health, finances, family members and our Christian walk. However, God is <u>Jehovah Nissi,</u> our Conqueror. If we follow the Lord, we will have victory. We must keep our trust in Him and Him alone. We must never rely on anything or anyone else to fight our battles.

There is no higher authority in this universe than God. There is no greater power in this universe than God. It is God who gives us the victory and always causes us to triumph. Because God reigns over all, we have confidence in a good outcome for any situation. We know that He is working everything out for our good.

FEARLESS

Because we belong to God, we have His covering and His protection. We understand that nothing and no one can harm us unless God allows it. The Bible says, "No weapon that is formed against thee shall prosper…" (**Is. 54:17 KJV**). Therefore, we don't have to walk around in fear and despair from things we see, feel and hear. Abba, (Father or Daddy), has sworn by His own self never to forsake us. We can live in the confidence of His Word and who He is. Instead of being sad, we can be glad. **The Bible** says that He will give us "…beauty for ashes, the oil of joy for mourning, the garment of praise for a spirit of heaviness…". (**Is.61:3 KJV**)

"Lift up your heads, O ye gates…" (**Ps. 24:7 KJV**) We should not walk around sad with bowed-down heads. Don't be afraid. **2Chron. 32:7 says KJV**, "Be strong and courageous; be not afraid or dismayed…for there are more with us than with him" (meaning with our enemy). So be joyful. "Clap your hands all ye people; shout unto God with a voice of triumph "(**Ps. 47:1 KJV**). There is no reason to fear.

8

NOT BY SIGHT

IF THIS-THEN THAT?

Most human beings operate based on a logical assumption of "if this, then that", which means, "if this is true, then that is true." This assumption is pretty accurate for most natural or physical situations. For example: if you touch the fire, you will get burned. One might say that is pretty simple and very obvious, and in most cases they would be right.

DON'T ASSUME

However, when we speak of spiritual situations, this assumption does not always hold true. **2Cor.5:7 KJV** says, "For we walk by faith, **not by sight.**" For instance, in the Bible, one plus one plus one equals ONE. God the Father, God the Son, and God the Holy Ghost make only One true and living God. Another example is five loaves of bread and three fish that fed more than five-thousand people. This happened after Jesus blessed the food and gave it to His disciples to distribute to the people. A third example is that after Jesus died on the cross and was buried, He rose again and is alive today.

THE WORD OF HIS POWER

In the beginning, God said "Let there be…", and it was. Things came into being after God said so. So, the reality of things is what God says it is. Jesus still upholds all things by the Word of His power.

NOT NATURAL

Because of God's compassion for us and love for us, He doesn't just leave us at the mercy of "nature" or natural things. His power is pre-eminent (or greater) than the natural scheme of things that He put into motion from the foundation of the world. God makes exceptions all the time to the rules of nature and science.

GOD'S GRACE

God, in His loving kindness and tender mercies towards us, intervenes in our circumstances to conform them to His will. We have to remember to trust in the Lord with all our hearts and lean not unto our own understanding. In all our ways, acknowledge Him, and He shall direct our paths. By God's grace, the laws of physics are overturned. The laws of biology are overridden. The laws of cause and effect are rendered null and void.

QUITE THE OPPOSITE

Little becomes much. The impossible becomes possible. What was meant for bad becomes for our good. It's not always what it looks like. God's grace outweighs doctors' reports, pink slips on the job, final notices in the mail, court proceedings or anything that would rob us of our peace. For God "is able to do exceeding abundantly above all that we ask or think, according to the power that worketh in us." (**Eph. 3:20 KJV**) "Greater is He that is in you than he that is in the world." (**1John 4:4 KJV**) We can't always go by what a situation looks like. Don't jump to conclusions before it's time. Wait on God.

9

NO COINCIDENCE

TIME AND SPACE

God has plans for our lives that are not limited by time and space. Everywhere is in His presence and in His power. Time does not control Him. He controls time. Time and space are under His authority, because it is He who made them. He is the God who was, and is and is to come, the God of past, present, and future. He knows beforehand what is going to happen, and He directs us to appointed <u>intersections</u> and divine <u>connections</u> that align with His plans. An intersection is where two things meet: roads, streets, places. It is where one crosses the path of another. A connection has to do with an interaction with another person.

A MAZE

God desires for us to make these <u>divine connections </u>with people by arriving at the appointed intersections (meeting places) at the appointed (predetermined) times. He has expected outcomes waiting for us if we keep our appointments. There are no coincidences in our lives. To us, life can feel like a maze that we are wondering through trying to find our way.

However, God views our lives from above looking down. He can see every turn in the maze, around every corner. He will direct our path, so that there are no surprises. We don't know which way to go, or what decisions to make. Unless we consult God, we are just guessing. God has good plans for us, but we need to trust Him and obey Him.

ORDERED STEPS

God knows all of the dangers that are waiting around the next bend in the road. When we ***miss*** the accident about to happen on the next street, or ***almost*** lose our purse or wallet, these things are not coincidences. We need to acknowledge that it is God who has caused us to miss these calamities. It is also God who moves us in the right direction to be blessed, for example, when we get that promotion or that unexpected check. God will order our steps and direct our path. "The steps of a good man are ordered by the Lord" (**Ps. 37:23 KJV**)

ON TIME

We need to realize when things happen to work out for us, run smoothly or give us favor, it is not by chance. It is not by accident, and it is not by luck. It is because of God's <u>divine order</u>. It is because we have arrived at the appointed intersection for the divine connection to take place. We are at the right place at the right time to meet the right people. We are in God's perfect will.

Timing is extremely important. It makes all the difference as to the place where we end up. For example: if you travel on a highway for ten minutes, you will not arrive at the same destination as if you travel that highway for two hours. We arrive on time at the appointed intersection (destination) to meet our divine connection for a foreordained result only if we listen to and obey God. God knows because He sees. He sees the entirety of our lives. He knows our end from our beginning.

A SET UP

If we understand that God continually desires to lead us into blessings, maybe we will be more apt to listen and obey His directions. Remember, there are no coincidences. Everything is planned. Everything is set up or orchestrated for our benefit. We must listen to the one who has it all arranged for us. Ask God for directions. He will guide us and show us the way, when to go, stop, turn or reverse.

10

WAIT ON GOD

WAIT ON GOD

God is a God of His Word because He cannot lie. "…Has He spoken, and shall He not make it good?" (**Numb. 23:19 KJV**) He watches over His Word to perform it. We can have every confidence that He will answer our prayers if we pray according to His will. When adverse situations in life occur, we must trust God to help us. He will hear our cries and deliver us. He has given us many precious promises. All of the promises of God in Christ are yes and Amen to the glory of God, but we must be willing to wait for their fulfillment, trusting that it will come to pass. "Wait, I say, on the Lord." (**Ps. 27:14 KJV**)

WAIT IN FAITH

As we wait on God, we need to wait in faith, <u>not in doubt</u>. For in doubt, we cannot receive anything from the Lord. **The Bible** says that we must believe that we receive the desires we pray for. We must have the faith to decide that we already possess them. We cannot control when God's hand will move. Our confidence has to be in the love that He has already shown us and in His faithfulness towards us.

Waiting can be difficult. We can experience weakness and even fretfulness sometimes, but we can cast our cares upon God for He cares for us. If we wait on the Lord and be of good courage, He will strengthen our hearts. We can be victorious against the devil's strategies (against discouragement, depression, doubt, and self-pity) by speaking and using (by faith) the whole armor of God, which is <u>His Word</u>.

WAIT IN HOPE

The Bible says that we have need of patience and perseverance in order to receive the promises of God. But are we waiting patiently? Or are we waiting in fear, in distress, in sadness? No, we should be waiting in hope and anticipation of the joy to come. We can rest in the Lord, and wait patiently for Him, being fully persuaded that He will act on our behalf. **Ps. 27:13 KJV** says, "I had fainted unless I <u>believed</u> to see the goodness of the Lord in the land of the living." We have to encourage ourselves and tell our souls to "hope thou in God". Put a smile on our faces, and say," I shall yet praise Him" **(Ps. 42:5 KJV)**, for He is my God. "My soul doth wait for Him, and in His Word do I <u>hope</u>". **(Ps. 130:5 KJV)**

We know that God is faithful, and He will <u>deliver</u> us out of all our afflictions because He is our Deliverer. "God is our Refuge and our Strength". **(Ps.46:1 KJV)** We don't have to be afraid. We don't have to be downtrodden. He is the lifter of our heads. He will give us beauty for ashes, joy for mourning and a praising heart for a heavy spirit. We can go to God in prayer, and His peace will keep our hearts and minds through Christ Jesus. "Weeping may endure for a night, but joy comes in the morning." **(Ps.30:5 AMP)** It is just a temporary situation that God will change. As Job said, let us also say, I will wait until my change comes.

FAITH <u>WITH</u> WORKS

"...Faith without works is dead". (**James 2:20 KJV**) If we believe it is going to rain, we will carry an umbrella. If we believe that the Lord will not withhold any good thing from us if we <u>walk</u> uprightly, we can believe to receive what we ask God for. To "walk" means <u>what we do</u> in our lives, how we behave. What is the use for anyone to profess to have faith if he has no good works to show for it? While we are waiting on God to bless us in our situation we should be acting in preparation and expectation of the blessing.

A nobleman gave his servants money and told them to work with that until he came back. Jesus says we are to <u>occupy</u> until <u>He</u> comes. Do what we can with what we have until He comes (into our situation). There should be <u>some works of faith</u> or actions we can take to reflect that we are expecting God to show up in our circumstances.

Examples of works of faith could be getting some training or education while we are waiting. Maybe it's working in a particular ministry of the local church or community, maybe saving money toward the vision, or cleaning out an area to make room for the vision. Maybe it's getting our house in order (literally), getting our spirit in order (studying and spending time with God), breaking some habits or some associations, changing how we think about others, or being consistent about getting our health in order.

We can be working while we are waiting, as we prepare to receive the answers to our prayers. Our works reveal <u>how</u> we are waiting on God and <u>what</u> we are really believing God for. We can rejoice through the suffering while we wait on the glory of God to be revealed.

11

THE WORK OF
THE MINISTRY

EFFECTIVE TOOLS

What is the work of the ministry? **The Bible** says that we are to be equipped (trained, educated) as tools for <u>the work of the ministry</u> that builds up Christ's Body, the church. The work we do is supposed to do this. This means that if we are doing the work right, the result should be that the Body of Christ is being built up. Being effective tools means that our work produces the desired effect.

DESIRED EFFECT

What does the desired effect look like? If we are effective, the Body of Christ is increased and strengthened. The Body of Christ becomes greater in maturity and unity. There is more love and compassion. They are encouraged and steadfast. Their faith is stronger. They walk in righteousness. They are humble and repentant. God is magnified in their lives, and their foundation is surer than ever before.

OUR FATHER'S BUSINESS

We need to be about our Father's business. That is, engaging in actions that will bring about these effects. We cannot do anything without the Holy Spirit. We need His leading and His empowering to achieve His goals. If we pray and ask Him, and if we live righteously, obedient to God in every way, Holy Spirit will grace us with His anointing to do the work of the ministry.

The (Holy) Spirit of the Lord was upon Christ and He anointed Him (Christ) for specific purposes. His purpose to preach (or proclaim) the gospel of good tidings to the poor should be our purpose too. We are anointed to do the same. The poor are anyone who is without Christ. We are to make them aware of their need for Christ through preaching, speaking, teaching and living Christ.

WORKING ON OURSELVES

What are you doing? Are you giving time and effort to the work of the ministry every day? How do you spend your time? How much of your 24-hour day do you participate in the work of the ministry...even if it's just building yourself up, for you too are part of the Body of Christ. It is needful to build ourselves up with reading and studying the Word, praying, meditating, worshipping and fasting. Give part of each day to building yourself up in your faith so that you can be a more useful and usable part of the Body of Christ.

THIS MEANS YOU

The work of the ministry is not exactly the same as the work of a minister. We are all to be participants in the work of the ministry, whether or not we have a title attached to our name. God gave all of us the ministry of reconciliation, which means bringing people into harmony with God by giving them the message of forgiveness and restoration. As this message is received, the Body of Christ is increased. So, this is not something to opt out of. As a Saint, this work is what we are to do as we are equipped to do so.

12

EVERLASTING LOVE

ENDURING LOVE

It is amazing to know that God will never run out of love for us. It is not because of how we act or what we've accomplished. He loves us in spite of who we are and what we've done. **Rom. 5:8 KJV** says that "God commended His love towards us in that while we were yet sinners, Christ died for us." This means that He showed or clearly proved His love for us by dying for us.

Jer. 31:3 KJV says, "…I have loved thee with an <u>everlasting love</u>…". This means that His love is *eternal, perpetual and continuing*. It is **eternal** in that it is outside of the confines (boundaries) of time. This includes past, present or future. In other words, He has always loved us, and nothing can change that. His love is **perpetual** because there is no end to it. His love is **continuing** to this day and forever.

It is encouraging to know that His love is not based on our ability to be perfect, even though he does command us to be holy for He is holy. His love is agape, unconditional. When we fall short, we can confess and repent and start over anew. He forgets our sins like they never happened.

He doesn't hold them against us. This is because His love is patient and forgiving. For the Lord is good, and His mercy endures forever.

UNCHANGING LOVE

When we find ourselves in strenuous situations, some that we may have caused ourselves, we can know that we are not left there alone. He is with us as Jehovah Shamah. "The Lord is there." (**Ezek. 48:35 KJV**) The Lord will bring us out with a mighty hand. He is our God, and He is our God forever. Because of His love, He will be there for us. **Josh.1:5** says, "I will be with thee. I will not fail thee." In **Isaiah 41:10,** God tells us not to be afraid. He says, "I am thy God. I will strengthen thee; yea, I will help thee; yea, I will uphold thee with the right hand of my righteousness." His love does not change.

LOVING KINDNESS

Jer. 31:3 KJV says "...with loving kindness have I drawn thee." God reaches out to us and draws us unto Himself with kindness motivated by deep and everlasting love. One of the ways He reaches out to us is through His Word. He gives us His Word to show us the way to live according to His will. He also reaches out to us with His actions. He has adopted us into His family. He planned beforehand for us to be adopted as His own. When we believe on Him, He gives us power to become His sons (children). This was His kind intention for us.

GREAT LOVE

What great love our Father extends towards us! In order to satisfy this great and wonderful and intense love with which He loved us, He has been rich in His mercy towards us. Even when we were dead in our sins, He hath made us alive in union with Christ. He saved us by grace (by unmerited favor) to sit down together with Him in heavenly places. He wants us to be with Him. "For God so loved the world that He gave His only begotten Son, that whosoever believeth in Him should not perish, but have everlasting life", which is life with Him. (**John 3:16 KJV**) How great is His love for us!

SACRIFICIAL LOVE

The Word says, "All have sinned and come short of the glory of God." (**Rom. 3:23 KJV**) "The wages of sin is death, but the gift of God is eternal life through Jesus Christ our Lord." (**Rom. 6:23 KJV**)

The sin debt needed to be paid, so

God sent His Son to die in our place. Jesus said to the Father, here I come in the volume of the book, to do thy will. Jesus said, Thou have prepared a body for Me to be an everlasting sacrifice for the sins of Your people.

Jesus paid the cost. He suffered, bled and died on the cross for our sins. He took the chastisement of our peace upon Himself. He was our substitute, the sacrificial Lamb that saved our lives. He was crucified, but He is risen and now seated in heaven on the right hand of the Father ever living to make intercession for us. Greater love hath no man than that he would lay down his life for his friends.

13

RENEWING OF YOUR MIND

Be Not Conformed

We are in the world but not of the world. God does not want us to live our lives like the world does. There should be some kind of definite distinction between the people of the world and the people of God. We should be able to be identified by this distinction. The way we carry ourselves, how we act, think and talk should be definite give a-ways. We are to operate in the fruit of the Spirit, the first one being love. The choices we make in our appearance, our conversations, and our actions should be a reflection of the God we serve.

Let's do a self- examination. Is there anything that is different about us compared to non-Christians? What about our dress? Is there appropriate modesty and self-respect in our choice of clothing and accessories? This applies to women and men. What about words and phrases we use? Would the listener conclude that we represent Jesus? Our words should respect ourselves and those who hear us. Let not gossip, profanity nor criticism be heard from our mouths.

But Be Ye Transformed

Instead of copying off of the world and its ways of doing things, we are to change our ways of thinking. We should no longer think as we used to think. We should no longer operate in our old ways. There should be a definite change.

Our friends and family will have to get used to the new "us". We are now new creations in Christ. Old things are passed away, and behold, all things have become new. Let them marvel at the changes as we begin to walk in the Spirit and let our lights shine. Hopefully, some may want to know more about Jesus- out of curiosity or out of a desire to experience that same change in their lives.

Let them observe our faithfulness to our Lord. Let them see that our values have changed. What was priority for us before is no longer our priority. Our priorities are toward spiritual things more than natural. Pleasing and obeying God has become our priority. We are no longer trying to impress people with outward things. We are only interested in a lifestyle of obedience and worship to God, and we are rewarded for that through God's many benefits.

By the Renewing Of Your Mind

To renew means to make anew, to reform, to make over, to start anew. "By" means "as a result of ". So, as a result of starting over again in how our minds think, we will have new thoughts, different thoughts. We will carry out new actions that come from these new thoughts. We can wipe the slate clean daily of old thoughts by reading and studying and listening to the Word of God. This is how we continually get rid of our old, wrong ways of thinking that led us into wrong actions.

We need to renew our minds daily to overcome the evil thoughts and imaginations that will try to come back. With the Word, we can cast down those wrong thoughts and bring them into captivity (as prisoners) to the obedience of Christ. In other words, the Word of God has the power to change, overcome or defeat any of its enemies.

That You May Prove

Then, we can discern, see, know and understand. When we experience this renewal, we'll know that it is nothing short of a miracle. It is through the power of God's Word that the proof, the evidence, shows up. We can say for ourselves that we don't talk the same, we don't go the same places, we don't do the same things as we used to. Only God could have the kind of power to affect us like that.

What Is That Good And Acceptable And Perfect

God's plans for us are good. They are for our welfare and for our peace. They are to give us hope for our future. Because God is perfect, and His love for us is perfect, His plans for us are also perfect.

When we see what obeying God's Word shows us, then we will see that God's Word is the only measure of perfection, and our obedience to it is the only thing that is acceptable to Him

Will Of God

God's Word is His will. We should delight (find joy and happiness) in doing God's will. **The Bible** says we will have many blessings if we will obey God's Word. It is God's will for us to receive instruction from His Word. His Word will rebuke and convict us of sin. It points out to us our errors, when we are acting contrary to His will. Through His Word, God shows us how to correct our errors (sins), and what will happen if we don't correct them. God wants us to be trained in how to conform or align ourselves to be in agreement with His thoughts and purposes. This is what renewing our mind with the Word will do.

14

FAITHFUL OVER A FEW

FAITHFUL

God spoke to His disciples in the parable of the three servants whom He had given money to. When they increased the amount He gave them, He said, Well done thou good and <u>faithful</u> (honorable and admirable) servant. "You have been <u>faithful and trustworthy</u> over a little; I will put you in charge of much." (**Matt.25:21AMP**) He was teaching us to use our time, talents and treasures diligently. Diligently means attentively and persistently. In other words, without becoming tired and without slacking off; without stopping. <u>Faithful</u> means reliable, trusted, constant. God wants us to be His faithful servants as we daily live out our salvation without someone being there to police us.

ALL ALONE

Are we faithful in private? How do we spend our time when we are all alone? When things are not going as well as we would like them to, do we become paralyzed and spend our time fretting and worrying? Or do we still worship our God? Do we become less faithful and less likely to be one who will stand and be a bold ambassador for Christ? We must not let self-pity set in. Feelings of loneliness and isolation can stagnate and paralyze us. If we are not careful, we will waste our precious time feeling sorry for ourselves.

FIGHT BACK

We must go on! God is looking to see the strength of our faith, even when no one else is around. We strengthen our faith through the Word of God. Strong faith produces steadfastness. Then we won't waiver but will be able to stand. When we spend our time being faithful in the faith, the Fruit of the Spirit is manifested. We must continue in the faith, working on our own Christian progress building ourselves up in our most Holy faith and adding to our faith even the more qualities of God. We should refuse to give in to spirits of depression and sadness. These only serve to increase doubt in us. We have to wear our spiritual blinders and have our faces set like a flint, unwilling to yield to the devil's thoughts.

A SECRET PLACE

There is a secret place. It is under the shadow of the Almighty [whose power no foe can withstand]. Neither the enemy nor his fiery darts can follow us there. The cares of this world cannot follow us there. This place is in the presence of the Almighty God, where there is fullness of joy and pleasures for evermore. If we find ourselves getting depressed, we can go to the secret place. If we find ourselves getting lonesome, we can go to the secret place. If we are getting bored, we can go to the secret place. The enemy has no power there. **The Bible** talks about "dwelling" there. We can live there, but it takes effort on our part. We have to faithfully, reach for it each day. Once we reach it, we'll find rest for our souls.

RULER OVER MUCH

When God sees that we are faithful to our daily diligence of working out our own salvation, He will enlarge our territory to include others. He will know that He can trust us to stay on the job and produce fruit that shall remain. God will give us stewardship over the well-being of others. We will become mentors, and teachers and ministers for the sake of others. If, however, God sees us give in to demonic spirits that paralyze our growth, then we will miss out on opportunities to advance His Kingdom and bring Him glory. So, be faithful—even when nobody sees you but God.

15

BE THOU PERFECT

CHRIST, OUR HEAD

In **Gen. 17:1 KJV**, God told Abraham to "walk before me, and be thou perfect". In this, He meant to habitually live or run along with Him. Running along suggests that we are to live in agreement with Him and His commandments. And then it says, "and be thou perfect". If we live in agreement (that is, in obedience) with His commands, we will be on the road to perfection.

We will be like Him. God is perfect. **Deut. 32:4 AMP** says, "He is the Rock, His work is perfect, for all His ways are law and justice. A God of faithfulness without breach or deviation, just and right is He".

Christ is our measure of perfection. Christ is the Head, and we are His body. We are spiritually attached to God. As His body, we are no less perfect than our Head. This is the <u>order</u> and <u>position</u> in which Christ has ordained the church to <u>function.</u>

PERFECT POSITION, PERFECT ORDER

The position of the Body denotes its <u>order</u>. It is under the Head and is therefore subject to the Head. We, as the Body of Christ, are subject to the will of Christ. We are His instruments to execute His will. Our agenda and purpose are whatever His agenda and purpose is. We are to be obedient to Him. In turn, He takes care of us and gives us directives.

As Christ's Body, we are in the perfect <u>order</u> that He has placed us. We are partakers of His divine (perfect) nature and are to be fruitful in the knowledge of Him. We should develop good character, spiritual understanding, alert discipline, passionate patience, reverent wonder, warm friendliness and generous love—each trait fitting into and developing the others. These are His qualities, which we have access to, and thus, the working of His perfection continues in us.

PERFECT FUNCTION

When Christ ascended to heaven, He was no longer physically in the earth. But, because He left the Holy Spirit to dwell within us, we are now empowered to continue His work and to do even greater works in the earth. Now we can impact people on a human level as we are directed by the Holy Spirit. What a perfect design!

Just as our minds direct our bodies, the mind of Christ, which we have, directs us to carry out His desires. In His Word, His thoughts, feelings and purposes are expressed. He directs by His Word just as our minds direct our physical bodies. He enables and equips us for whatever activity is needed to carry out His plans. The primary purpose of our faculties and abilities is to carry out God's will.

As individuals, we have not attained to the measure of the stature of Jesus Christ. But we depend on God, who is faithful, to complete our calling as individuals. However, as His Body, we can function as He designed us to function—because of our connection to Him. Our connection is through the Holy Spirit, who is our guide and our teacher.

As His Body, we stand in an awesome place. We are part of Him. He has designed us to function as ONE with Him and with each other. That is the perfection that we are to walk in.

16

A WORD OF KNOWLEDGE

SUPERNATURAL INFORMATION

Have you ever had a vision from God? Not a vision of the future, but a vision of the present, one that pertains to present circumstances. This might be **a word of knowledge** from the Holy Spirit. Holy Spirit can give us knowledge for a specific situation at a given time. He simply imparts to us some of God's all-knowing information to help us for that particular situation. It is supernatural revelation of certain facts in the mind of God.

TO MINISTERS

A word of knowledge can come in a vision to ministers, as with the Apostle John on the Isle of Patmos. His vision was about the condition of the seven churches in Asia Minor.

TO LAY PEOPLE

The word of knowledge can also be given to "lay" people, people that don't hold any title in ministry. The Lord can show us specifically what is happening in a given moment in a situation that we know nothing about.

CURRENT EVENTS

Holy Spirit can speak to us the truth about a present fact that we are not aware of. (Acts 10:19 KJV) This is the gift of the word of knowledge. However, this happens only according to His (Holy Spirit's) will. Its manifestation is totally controlled by Him.

TO FIND LOST PROPERTY

The gift of the word of knowledge can help us find lost property. Have you ever not been able to find something, even after spending much time looking for it? In frustration, you may have given up and just prayed to God for help and put it out of your mind. Many times, that is when Holy Spirit will show you exactly where to look, and when you obeyed, you found your lost object.

TO ENCOURAGE US

God can give a word of knowledge to encourage us. Just when we are feeling down and discouraged, God can give us a word of knowledge (or vision) that pertains to our present situation that will cheer us up and encourage us.

TRUTH ABOUT PEOPLE

God can give us a word of knowledge concerning the real hearts of people. He can also enable us to avoid dangers and traps by giving us a word of knowledge about which routes to avoid.

WHAT TO PRAY FOR

God can give us a word of knowledge about what to pray for. Sometimes Holy Spirit will tell us to pray right then for someone's deliverance, healing or victory in a specific situation.

Because the word of knowledge always brings revelation of a present situation, timeliness is necessary. It is important to take immediate action. Procrastination or postponing action will nullify the power that was available for that moment. The anointing is for that particular time of our obedience to Him.

When God says "go" or "do" something, He means NOW...not later when it is more convenient for you.

DO SOMETHING

Sometimes, we can only take a step in response to what God has told or shown us. We should take that step. Sometimes, God may only reveal a step at a time. When He does, we need to "act", and then wait in faith for further directions.

We have to remember that it's at God's timing and the Holy Spirit's will that information is given to us. We should not try to go further with the vision on our own. There is no anointing for that.

17

AN ABUNDANCE OF RAIN

ANSWER TO PRAYER

We have prayed for rain, and God has heard us. Although no clouds may be visible at this time, "there is a sound of abundance of rain". (**1 Kings 18:41 KJV**) **Rain** represents provisions and new life. We can be encouraged that the drought has ended. We know that the Lord, He is God. He is the sovereign King. There is no God beside Him. We know that it is He who has brought us through the drought, for He is able to do exceeding abundantly above all that we ask or think. We thank Him for the answer to our prayers.

A LIGHTER LOAD

In the natural, rain falls freely and easily without hindrance and without struggle. The rain brings nourishment to that which is alive and gives life to that which would live. It brings a sweet smell to the air. It washes away dirt and smog and leaves us with fresh clean air to breathe and to renew our strength.

<u>Spiritually</u>, when God sends the rain, it clears the atmosphere of hindrances. All of a sudden, doors of opportunity and favor swing wide open. Instead of trudging along pushing through barriers, suddenly, we are standing on a free-moving floor (like in an airport). We have access to what was out of our reach before. Obstacles have been removed, and our desires and needs are coming to us. It becomes easier to reach our goals, and the burden feels lighter to carry. Deliverance has come.

A NEW SEASON

The season has changed. There is a newness and refreshing in the falling rain that will wash away the harshness of the season that is past. When God sends the rain, we can breathe a sigh of relief and have contentment. A change has come. God will meet our needs and multiply our blessings to be even greater than we had before.

IN EXPECTATION

We were expecting God to provide for us. We did not quit. We knew that He would equip and enable us to carry out the vision He has given us. We read the vision that was written and made plain for us. Then, we began to run with the vision to execute it. Knowing that the vision is for an appointed time we remained in patient expectation of its manifestation. The time has come.

BE READY

It may not look like rain, but the rain is coming. We have to be ready. We have followed all of God's instructions carefully and faithfully. We remained with one accord in unity and love. We prepared ourselves as God directed us to do. We stayed on task. Everyone is in place and engaged in doing the work of the ministry.

IN A LITTLE WHILE

<u>Then, in a little while</u>, the great rain came. The time that seemed so long in coming and so difficult to wait for was only a little while in God's eyes. For with the Lord, a thousand years is as one day. God will establish, strengthen, and settle us after we have suffered <u>a little while.</u> Then, it will be like a woman who soon forgets the pain of childbirth after gazing in the eyes of her healthy baby. Forgetting those things which are behind, we will press forward and focus on the new possibilities that God has opened for our future.

18

COMPLETING YOUR CALLING

MADE BY GOD

Did you ever wonder what your purpose in life was? Was it to be a parent, a spouse, a fantastic employee or businessperson? Actually, your purpose in life is what God says it is. It is He who made us, and not we ourselves. So our purpose is not what we make it, but it is what God has meant for us all along. Each of us is a specific instrument for God's specific purpose. Our life is following a particular pattern foreseen and laid out by God. There is a method in what may seem to be the "madness" of our lives.

CALLED BY GOD

We, who love God, are the called of God according to His purpose. He called us with a holy calling, saved us and gave us a purpose and grace in Christ Jesus before the world began. He foreordained us to be adopted as His own children. His intention for us was kind and good, for our welfare and to the praise of His glory. God chose us from the foundations of the world, that we should be holy (consecrated and set apart), for Him.

KNOWN BY GOD

If any person truly loves God, He is known by Him and owned by Him, worthy of His intimacy and love. God knows each of us. "Even the very hairs on our head are all numbered". (**Luke 12:7 KJV**) Nothing is hidden from God. God sees all. He knows what we have done and what we will do. God has made us fearfully and wonderfully complex. He saw us and what we were made of and wrote in a book all the days of our life before they even took place. God knows all of our ways, even our thoughts.

EQUIPPED BY GOD

God knows what He has called us to be, and He equips us for that calling. He knows what it will take for each of us to be formed to the pleasure of His will. God will make us what we ought to be and equip us with everything good that we may carry out His will. God, Himself, works in us and accomplishes that which is pleasing in His sight through Jesus Christ.

COMPLETED BY GOD

Only God knows what kinds of experiences are needed to bring us into the place which He has ordained for us—our expected end. God uses our experiences and choices in life to conform us to His will and His plans for us. **The Bible** says in Rom.8:29-30 to be molded into the image of His Son. **The Bible** says we were not only foreordained, but also called, justified (made righteous), glorified (raised to a heavenly state of being).

Our faith is tested and proven when we suffer trials and temptations. So yes, God does purposely allow trials to come, in His method of preparing us for what He has planned for us. Knowing this, we can go through them with joy, peace, and expectation for a positive finish. Many are the afflictions of the righteous, but God delivers them out of them all. "Now thanks be unto God, which always causes us to triumph in Christ Jesus". **(2Cor.2:14 KJV)**

Not only to realize what our purpose is, but to actually be able to walk in it, is the ultimate satisfaction in life. It is good to know that <u>God will complete His calling</u> in our lives. "And I am convinced and sure of this very thing, that He who began a good work in you will continue until the day of Jesus Christ [right up to the time of His return], developing [that good work]and perfecting and bringing it to full completion in you." **(Phil.1:6 AMP)**

19

WALKING IN HOLINESS

HOLY SPIRIT IN US

When we confess and believe Christ as our Savior, His Spirit comes to dwell within us. His Spirit is the Holy Spirit or Holy Ghost. It is Christ's presence in us. However, just because we have the Holy Ghost in us does not make us automatically holy. Holiness is not something that just happens or a badge that we wear. It is not something that can be taken for granted. It is our actions in response to the prompting or leading of the Holy Spirit within us.

HOLY ON PURPOSE

God tells His people to, "Be ye holy for I am holy" (**!Pet.1:16**). Because He tells us to "be holy" means that we have that ability. We can <u>will ourselves</u> to be holy. We can decide to be holy on purpose. Being holy is not only conducting ourselves with **true reverence**, but it also includes our state of mind (set and made up) to obey God. "As (a man) thinketh in his heart, so is he." (**Pro 23:7 KJV**) So, we need to have holiness in our thoughts as well as in our actions. Holy thoughts lead to holy behavior.

SEEING GOD

Obedience to the Word of God will make us holy. **The Bible** talks about holiness as sanctification. Jesus is asking God to <u>purify, consecrate and separate us</u> (make us holy) <u>by His truth</u>. "Thy Word is truth." (**John 17:17 KJV**) In God's Word, we learn that a right relationship with God leads to right relationships with each other. We should make every effort to live in peace with all men. Sin is neglecting to follow God's Word. God has no fellowship with sin. Sin blocks our vision of God, as did the curtain block the view and access to the Arc of the Covenant from all the people-except the consecrated priests. The Arc of the Covenant is where the priests would meet with God. With Jesus' sacrificial death, the curtain (veil) was torn giving us personal access to God's presence, but we must repent of all our sins in order to have fellowship with Him. Only he who has clean hands and a pure heart can enter the Most Holy place. "Blessed are the pure in heart for they shall see God". (**Matt.5:8 KJV**)

CONTROLLED BY HOLY SPIRIT

No unbeliever can walk in holiness. Holiness is the nature of the Holy Ghost. It's who He is. He is the source of holiness for a believer.

Having the Holy Ghost and following the leading of the Holy Ghost are not the same thing. The difference is in being controlled by the Holy Spirit and seeking those things that He desires. Holiness is letting Holy Spirit have His way, doing those things which gratify Him, not ourselves.

If we live in the Spirit, let us also walk in the Spirit, having our conduct controlled by the Spirit. The fruit of the Spirit are these: love, joy, peace, longsuffering, gentleness, goodness, faith, meekness and temperance. Are these fruit evident in our lives? If we walk and live habitually in the Holy Spirit, we will not fulfill the lusts of the flesh (the desires of human nature without God).

CHOICES

You can be saved and not necessarily holy. Holiness shows up in the way we live our lives and in the choices we make. Will we choose what pleases our old nature or what pleases Holy Spirit? We have a regenerated, born again new nature. **2Cor.5:17 KJV** says, "…Old things are passed away, and behold all things are become new." Every day we can choose to follow the Word of God and the Holy Spirit.

20

LIVING OUT THE TRUTH

MISSING THE MARK

Have you ever been frustrated with yourself for repeating the same sins over and over—though not intentionally? Maybe it's in your <u>speech</u>, perhaps speaking a criticizing word. Maybe it's in your <u>thoughts</u>, a doubtful, rebellious or unkind thought. Maybe in <u>actions</u>, when you **omit** or don't do something or don't go somewhere that you know you should have. Or possibly when you **commit** (or engage in) something that God is not pleased with. Well, if you love God, you become not only convicted, but sorry and disappointed in yourself that you have displeased God again. **John 8: 34 AMP** says that "whoever commits, and practices sin is the slave of sin."

KNOWLEDGE OF THE TRUTH

Just because we study and gain knowledge of the truth and understand the truth is not a guarantee that we are living out the truth. **John 17:17 KJV** says, "Thy Word is truth". Even if we know the truth (the Word), are we free to live out the truth? The Bible says in John 8:34, we shall know the truth, and **the truth shall make us free**. Jesus Himself is the truth that sets us free. Who the Son sets free shall be free indeed.

A FREE SPIRIT AND BODY

What is hindering our freedom to live out the truth? **The Bible** says, the good that I want to do I don't do, but the evil which I desire not to do is what I do. Christ died to set us free from sin. But our bodies remain subject to the longings of our carnal nature. However, sin shall not have dominion over us. In other words, we can bring our bodies under subjection and not yield to sin. Our old nature was crucified with Christ, so that our body (which is the instrument of sin) should no longer serve sin. (We can stand in the power (the grace) that Christ gives us and refuse to be entangled again with the bondage of slavery to sin.

GO TO WAR

There is a war between the spirit and the flesh. When we want to do good, evil is always right there with us trying to captivate our minds. We can protect ourselves with the whole armor of God, which He provides. We can cast down those imaginations (wipe them out) and replace them with God's Word. This is how we **fight to live out God's truth**.

OUR WEAPON IS THE WORD

We should stay focused on the Word of God. Let it dwell in us richly. Speak the Word, think the Word, and live the Word. In other words, keep His Word in our mouths, in our minds and in our hearts, so we can do it. Think Godly thoughts. We do what we think.

Love the Lord with all thy heart, soul, mind and strength. Love thy neighbor as thyself. These are His two most important commands. We can live out the truth by letting this **love** dictate our actions. Concerning speech, His Word says, "let no corrupt communication proceed out of your mouth…" (**Eph. 4:29 KJV**) Concerning <u>thoughts</u>, His Word says, "…if there be any virtue, and if there be any praise, think on these things." (**Phil. 4:8 KJV**)

God has given us everything we need to win the war. So let us not be content only to know the truth, but let us stand in our freedom to live out the truth victoriously every day of our lives. "But **be ye doers of the Word** and not hearers only, deceiving yourselves." (**James 1:22 KJV**)

21

THE WORD BECAME FLESH

JESUS IS THE WORD

"In the beginning was the Word, and the Word was with God, and the Word was God." (**John 1:1 KJV**) "And the Word was **made flesh** and **dwelt among us** and we **beheld His glor**y, the glory as of the only begotten of the Father, full of grace and truth." (**John 1:14 KJV**) In John's vision, he sees Christ returning as Warrior, Messiah and King, "and the title by which He is called is The Word of God." (**Rev. 19:1 AMP**)

"But when the fullness of the time was come, God sent forth His Son, made (born) of a woman, made under the law" (of natural birth). (**Gal. 4:4 KJV**) The *Word Became Flesh* means that Christ went from a spiritual existence in heaven to a natural existence in earth. He went from invisible to visible. He stepped out of heaven and walked the earth.

OUR EXAMPLE

How can the Word become flesh today? We are to follow Christ's example and let the "Word" become flesh in us. If we read it, and it stays on the page, it is dead letter, without life. If we speak it or hear it without receiving it <u>into our spirit</u>, or letting it become a part of who we are, it is dead letter, without life. Only as we are <u>obedient</u> to the Word through <u>faith</u> does it create for us newness of life. (John 6:33) The Word activated in us by faith will produce change in our spirit, soul, and body that Demonstrates God's will. Then we can be the living Word, as Jesus was, that becomes flesh (becomes alive), and <u>dwells among us</u> (the people of earth).

BEHELD HIS GLORY

We **beheld** His **glory**. "<u>Beheld</u>" means we saw (observed) with our own eyes. As we dwell among the people of earth, we demonstrate God's Word in our everyday lives, and we make it easy for others <u>to behold</u> (or see) who He is. His glory can be seen. "<u>His glory</u>" is His honor, His majesty. If we let our lights so shine that men may see our good works, they will recognize, honor and praise the Father which is in heaven. Then we can truly be living epistles (or letters) by being a living example and making the ways of God clearly understood.

GRACE AND TRUTH

Jesus, as the Word, is full of <u>grace and truth</u>. Grace is God's unmerited favor and loving-kindness, which we are partakers of. Jesus is the truth. As we walk in God's grace, we should live a life of truthfulness, that is, a life that lives out the Word. The Word must become a part of who we are.

LIFE IN THE WORD

We must let the life in the Word influence and control our lives. It can do many things for us if we let it. "Through the Word we are put together and shaped up for the tasks God has for us." (**2Tim.3:17 MSG**) The Word will train us to live God's way, showing us truth, exposing our rebellion and correcting our mistakes. God's Word is alive and full of power. It is ready and able to move in us.

His Word can <u>become flesh</u> in each of us. If it becomes part of our personality, part of our character, it becomes alive in us. We receive the life of the Word into our spirits, and it quickens our souls. It begins to activate itself in our hearts, transforming us, growing us, establishing us, grounding us in the truth and producing the fruit of itself in us. We are no longer the same.

22

GOD WITH US

EMMANUEL

We, as believers, can walk in this world with confidence and boldness. We have the assurance of God's presence with us. If we realize that wherever we go, in whatever the circumstances may be, we are never by ourselves, spiritually. With or without our friends or family, we are never alone. We never have to be intimidated by anything in this life, for our God is **with** us.

God, Himself, came to earth to be among us. "Behold, a virgin shall be with child, and shall bring forth a son, and they shall call his name Emmanuel, which being interpreted is, God **with** us." (**Matt.1:23 KJV**) **With** us means that God <u>accompanied</u> us, that He is <u>by</u> us, <u>close to</u> us, that we are <u>together</u>. It means that He is <u>for</u> us, that He is <u>pro</u> us, He is in <u>our behalf</u>.

OUR STANDBY

After Jesus physically returned to heaven, He left His Spirit to remain here to dwell in us and stand by us.

We are in good company on this journey in Christ. Although there are demonic powers in the earth at work against us, the power of God is far above them all. Plus there are more that are with us than that are with them. This makes us confident and triumphant knowing that whatever we go through, whatever we may have to do, it is with the knowledge that we have help, back-up and support. Not only is Holy Spirit in us, but God is also **with** us.

I AM THAT I AM

God's presence and everything that He presents is **with** us at all times. In **the Bible**, Jesus says, **I Am with** you always. Even if we don't feel Him, it is a fact that He is always **with** us. In **Heb.13:5-6 AMP** God says, "I will not in any way fail you nor give you up nor leave you without support. I will not, I will not, I will not in any degree leave you helpless, nor forsake, nor let you down (relax my hold on you)! Assuredly not! And, we can be encouraged by this and boldly say, "the Lord is my helper, and I will not fear what man shall do to me." Again, in **Is 41:10**, God tells us "**I Am with** thee", **I Am** thy God, I will strengthen you, I will help you, I will uphold you…" Uphold means to sustain, maintain, and retain. In other words, He will KEEP us. How will He do this? He will do it by His power, and by everything that He presents as God, which is every part of His nature.

ALL THAT HE PRESENTS

One of the things that He presents as God is His peace. **John 14:27 KJV** says, "…my peace I give unto you." Circumstances don't make us to have anxiety. God gives us His peace for any situation. We are not to be anxious about anything because God's peace shall KEEP our hearts and minds through Christ Jesus.

Also, God **with** us presents His <u>grace.</u> For He is the God of all grace. We have the freedom to come boldly to His throne of grace, obtain mercy and find grace to help us in the time of need.

God **with** us is our shield and our protector. "The Lord is my rock, and my fortress, and my deliverer; my God, my strength, in whom I will trust; my buckler, and the horn of my salvation, and my high tower." (**Ps.18:2 KJV**)

He is our <u>provider</u> and our <u>guide</u>. He is our <u>company-keeper</u>. In Him we have confidence and true companionship. He <u>looks out for us</u>. He has given His angels charge over us. We can cast all of our care upon Him for He <u>cares for us</u>. We can stand strong in the truth that God is **with** us.

23

THE LOVE OF MONEY

PROSPERITY PREACHING

Regarding prosperity preaching, **Ecc. 10:19 KJV** says, "... money answereth all things". This is not a biblical fact, but a statement of the belief of some neglectful people that have strayed from the faith. They believe their money can solve everything and provide whatever they want. They throw money after problems that they have created by their own lack of effort and lack of diligence. Then they think that that will make the problems go away, but it doesn't.

There are also those that believe "...that **godliness (or righteousness)** is a source of profit, a money-making business", and that financial prosperity is its goal. "We are to stay away from such people, but we are to pursue righteousness, faith, love, patience and meekness.

NOT THE ANSWER

Money does not answer all things. People who disagree with this idolize money. They trust in money rather than God. Money is dangerous because it deceives us into thinking that wealth is the easiest way to every solution.

Those who crave to be rich fall into temptation and a trap that leads to many foolish and harmful desires. They will self-destruct in no time. "For the love of money is the root of all evil." (**1Tim.6:10 KJV**) Greed leads to marriage problems, robbery, blow-ups in partnerships, and most of all, to the denial and turning away from God's truth.

THE PURSUIT OF HAPPINESS

The truth is **"...godliness with contentment is great GAIN"**. (1Tim. 6:6 **KJV**) This is where the real prosperity is. (AMP) It is the key to happiness. We should honor God and center our desires on Him, and we should be content with what God is doing in our lives. "For **GOD** is able to make all grace (every favor and earthly blessing) come to you in abundance, so that you may always and under all circumstances... be self-sufficient possessing enough ...for every good work and charitable donation." (**2Cor. 9:8 AMP**) If we learn to be just as content with little as with much, we have the secret of facing every situation. God knows what we have need of, and He is faithful to provide if we seek Him first.

THE WEALTHY

It is true that God gives us power to obtain wealth. However, those who are rich carry a great responsibility. They should not be arrogant nor put their hopes in wealth, but should put their hopes in God, who provides everything for our enjoyment. They are to do good and be charitable in helping others with compassion and generosity. If they do this, they'll build a treasure that is a good foundation for the future, so that they may lay hold of eternal life. "Lay not **up** for yourselves **treasures up** on earth, where moth and rust doth corrupt, and where thieves break through and steal: But **lay up** for yourselves tre**asures** in heaven, where neither moth nor rust doth corrupt, and where thieves do not break through nor steal. "**(Matt. 6:19-20 KJV)**

GOD VS. MONEY

No man can serve two masters. Loving one God, you'll end up hating the other. You cannot serve both God and money. Do not worry about what you will eat, drink or wear. Life is more than that.

We need to be fully absorbed with seeking God's Word, God's will, and God's provisions for our life. Then He will do exceeding abundantly above that which we could ever imagine.

24

TREASURE IN EARTHEN VESSELS

IN THE BEGINNING

Gen. 1:1-3 says that in the beginning, the earth was without form and void, and darkness was upon the face of the deep, and GOD SAID, "Let there be light, and there was light". **(Gen.1:3 KJV)** God's Word caused light to manifest in darkness. "…God is light, and in Him is no darkness at all." **(1John 1:5 KJV)** God called us out of darkness into His marvelous light. "For ye were (once) darkness, but now are ye light in the Lord…" **(Eph.5:8 KJV)** In **John 8:12 KJV**, Jesus said, "I am the light of the world; he that followeth me shall not walk in darkness, but shall have the light of life. God has given us the ministry of reconciliation whereby we share with others the light that His Word brings.

For God, who commanded the light to shine out of darkness, hath shined in our hearts, to give the light of the knowledge of the glory of God in the face of Jesus Christ." (2Cor. 4:6 KJV) In other words, in the face of (*close relationship with*) Jesus Christ, we find the knowledge of the glory of God (***the light** that shines in our hearts*). Therefore, since we have (*been given*) this ministry (*of reconciliation*), as we have received mercy (*to walk in the light*), we faint not (*to share it*). We will be faithful to fulfill it.

THIS TREASURE

2Cor. 4:7 KJV "But we have this treasure in earthen vessels…" This treasure, which **brings light** to our souls, is the doctrine of the gospel of Christ. It is the belief in and the ability to perceive that Jesus Christ is the Son of the living God, who was born, who lived, healed, saved souls, died on the cross, was buried and raised from the dead for our sakes. The most valuable thing (**treasure**) that any man can possess is the light of the gospel.

EARTHEN VESSELS

We have this glorious "treasure **in earthen vessels…**" or clay pots, our bodies. We were formed out of the dust. God put the most valuable treasure in a common vessel (made of clay) in order that mankind would not begin to exalt the vessel (himself) but would instead exalt the contents of the vessel (the work of God). That's why Paul said in **2Cor. 4:5 KJV, "We preach not ourselves, but Christ Jesus the Lord…"**

THE EXCELLENCY OF THE POWER

(2Cor.4:7 KJV) "…that the excellency of the power may be of God, and not of us." When God, through us, pours forth His love to the world around us, all of the glory belongs to Him because all of the power comes from Him. The excellency (or superiority) of the power which empowers us to be witnesses and ambassadors for Christ, and which transforms hearts and souls, is of God. We must not take any credit or bows for any influence that the Holy Spirit of God (working through us) has on anyone. It is only us yielding to the Holy Spirit. We have to make sure that the focus is never on us, but upon God, by whose mercy, we are privileged to carry out His work.

TO GOD BE THE GLORY

We must never get exalted in ourselves but must always humble ourselves under the mighty hand of God, and He shall exalt us in due time. We are but clay pots in the potter's hand. We must remember that the focus is no longer just God's work in us, but the focus is also God's work through us. It is our responsibility to resist the temptation to focus attention on self, **"...that the abundant grace might through the thanksgiving of many redound to the glory of God"**, (**2Cor. 4:15 KJV**) so that He alone might be glorified.

25

EVERY GOOD AND PERFECT GIFT

ROBBING GOD

James 1:17 KJV - "Every **good gift and every perfect gift** is from above, **and** cometh down from the Father of lights, with whom is no variableness, neither shadow of turning.

Did you ever think that you would steal God's glory? Have you ever thought to yourself or even said to someone, "Look what I have done? Aren't I great? Aren't I anointed? According to the scripture, any good thing, any excellent thing, any pure thing is a gift from God. Every grace and every blessing is a gift from God.

GOOD AND PERFECT THING

What does that mean, 'good and perfect thing'?

It is not referring only to an object. It also refers to our actions, appearances, presentations, accomplishments, achievements, ministrations…natural and spiritual. Anything in your life that is good, well or right is **from God**. "…For there is none good but one, that is, God." (**Mk. 10:18 KJV**) What does right mean? Right means anything that brings God glory.

TEMPTATION TO BRAG

Do you ever find yourself bragging or taking compliments for things that you would not have if not for God's graciousness? The truth is everything good that you have is from God. This includes your good character traits, your looks, your skills you have acquired, the abilities you were born with, knowledge you have gained, wisdom, insight, discernment, and the fruit of the Spirit. We can't brag on anything. **John 15:5 KJV** says, "I am the vine, ye are the branches: He that abideth in me, and I in him, the same bringeth forth much fruit: for without me ye can do nothing."

EXAMPLE

I remember a very specific time when I was complimented on my appearance at work. I stopped short of beaming with a big smile and taking a bow, which I was tempted to do because my goal is always to look my best at work. But then Holy Spirit brought to my mind how I had been fumbling around that morning, not really feeling confident about what I ended up wearing…because of some basic self-consciousness about how my clothes fit and the total look of professionalism that I desired.

Suddenly, with a sincere face I responded, "**anything right** that you see here (pointing to myself), **is God.**" I had then a very clear revelation that the positive end results were not of my own making, but they were because of the mercy and grace of God.

Have you ever found yourself in a situation that could have ended in a negative but ended up positive and asked yourself 'how did this happen? The answer is, it wasn't your doing. It was God!

CORRECT RESPONSE

We have to remember that God is in charge. He deserves all the glory and praise for every good and perfect thing. So if we are complimented or praised for anything, before we gloat with pride or take any bows, let us give glory to whom glory is due. "Give unto the Lord the glory due unto His name." (**Psalm 96:8 KJV**)

Before we thank the person for his kindness in speaking the compliment, we need to be saying, "Praise the Lord", or "Thank God", or "Glory be to God", for example. For, it is God who is the source of everything good and everything perfect.

26

CASTING CROWNS

AT THE THRONE

In Revelation chapter four, John shares with us the vision in heaven of the throne of God. The throne of God was surrounded by twenty-four other thrones on which sat the twenty-four elders representing the heavenly council, which are all of God's people. Also, before the throne were four living creatures representing the characteristics of God. His majesty and power were represented by a <u>lion</u>, His faithfulness, by an <u>ox</u>, His intelligence, by a <u>man,</u> and His sovereignty, by an <u>eagle</u>. These creatures **led the council** and thousands of thousands of people from every nation in heavenly **praises to God.**

IN THE SPIRIT

John says he was in the Spirit on the Lord's Day when he saw a vision and heard Jesus speaking to him. "In the Spirit" means he was absorbed in the power of the Holy Ghost. In the Spirit is where we also find the throne of God. It's where we go to worship Him and His majesty. It's where He can speak to us, counsel us, guide us, and reveal to us things that He wants us to know. It is a place where we can worship Him in Spirit and in truth.

FOUR AND TWENTY ELDERS

What did they do? **Rev.4:8 KJV** says that they "…rest not day and night, saying Holy, Holy, Holy. Lord God Almighty, which was and is and is to come." Because they represent us (the people of God), this tells us that we also should never cease worshipping and praising Our God. **The twenty-four elders fall down before Him who sits on the throne and worship Him. Worship** means to ascribe worth or worthiness to **God.** "They fall down before Him that sat on the throne, and worship Him that liveth for ever and ever, and <u>cast their crowns</u> before the throne, saying, Thou art worthy, O Lord, to receive glory and honor and power: for thou hast created all things, and for thy pleasure they are and were created ". (**Rev 4:10-11** **KJV**).

WHY CAST THEIR CROWNS

Casting their crowns means that they threw them down before Jesus. The significance of this move comes from an old Roman custom in which lesser Kings of local territories would show due respect to the Emperor, who was over the entire country. These kings were at times commanded to come before the Emperor and lay their crowns down before him in homage. The twenty-four elders cast their crowns before the Lord as a declaration of His worthiness to receive all the glory and honor and power, and not themselves.

CASTING YOUR CROWNS

Rev. 5:10 KJV, "thou hast made us unto our God <u>kings </u>and priests: and we shall reign on the earth." Have you learned to cast your crown at the Savior's feet yet? Just like the elders in heaven, we cannot worship the Lord while we are on our own thrones. Like them, we need to fall down, free ourselves from everything that hinders us, including spirits of pride and religious spirits, and give full honor and worship to Our God. That means rid our spirits of everything that exalts itself against the knowledge of God. God is waiting for a sweet-smelling savor to come up to His nostrils from each one of our voices blending together as an untainted offering of majestic praise. Like the elders, let us be with one accord, without distraction… with our only purpose of giving honor to Our God, who alone is worthy.

27

LIVING IS CHRIST

TO ME

"For to me to live is Christ, and to die is gain." Phil.1:21 KJV talks about what living is to a believer. For to me to live is Christ [His life in me], and to die is gain [because I'm finally free from sin]. Those of us who have professed our belief in Christ have a particular outlook on what life means to us. Spiritually speaking, we have new life once we are saved. According to **the Bible,** we must be born again, that is born of God. So that for us, living is "living His life in us".

TO LIVE IS CHRIST

God gave us the very life of Christ and quickened us (made us alive) with the same new life with which He quickened Christ. We became altogether new creatures in Christ Jesus. We are God's own handiwork, recreated, born anew, in Christ to do good works which He planned for us to do.

"**To live is Christ**" means to live out the plan and purpose that God has for our lives, to live in reverence, love and obedience to Him, to exemplify Him, His will and His nature, in all we do.

ALL THAT PERTAINS TO LIFE AND GODLINESS

Living is an attribute of Christ for He is the only true and living God. He is our life, and life came from Him.

According to **the Bible** knowing God is the key to all things that <u>pertain</u> to life and godliness. "Pertain" means things that relate to it, things that are connected to it, things that belong to life and godliness. In **John 10:10 KJV**, Jesus said, "I am come that they might have life, and that they may have it more abundantly." All things that have any relation to, and influence upon, the **true spiritual life and power of godliness** are from Jesus Christ. We were given this power when He called us to this life in Him. We must give diligence to make our calling sure and use this power to escape from the moral decay of the world, including its sins and pitfalls.

PRECIOUS PROMISES

Not only has God given us power, God has also given us many, many precious promises which protect us and guide us in this world. "For all the promises of God in Him (that is, <u>in Christ</u>) are yea, and in Him Amen, unto the glory of God by us." (**2Cor. 1:20 KJV**)

TO DIE IS GAIN

"...And to die..." means that our natural life leaves our physical bodies and our physical bodies return to dust. Then our spirits become absent from the body, and present with the Lord. Our **gain** will be **a glorified body, the presence of our Lord, and the absence of sin** because in the presence of God, there is no sin. There <u>we will be through with sin forever and ever.</u>

This will be our **full salvation.** Then we will be delivered (saved) from the burden of these physical bodies, which are subject to the senses of pain, lust and sickness. Then, we will be delivered from worries, disappointments and defeats and will no longer be prey for the devil's traps.

Instead, we will be in the presence of God **completely free** to **forever** worship Him. We will have the final victory. There will be no more crying, no more graves, no more fear of death, for it shall be destroyed.

28

SEAL OF OWNERSHIP

BORN OF GOD

How do <u>you know</u> you are your parents' child? Is it because you look like them? Is it because you have the same last name? Is it because you look like your siblings? Or is it because you live with them? These things <u>could</u> indicate that you are their child. But, what about foster children? They live in the house but have very different parents. In the physical church, there are people who are in the building, but not in the family of God. We come into the family of God by "spiritual birth", being born of God.

PERSONAL RELATIONSHIP

It's good to be a part of a family and to feel you are included in the family group. However, what means more to us are the moments of personal interactions between us and our parents. Maybe it is a memory of a time when your parent taught you a particular skill: For example, baking cookies, or changing a tire.

EVIDENCE OF AFFECTION

Even though it's comforting and reassuring to hear from others that you are "so-and-so's" kid, it's even more satisfying to hear your parent say "you are mine, and I love you", as a 1 on 1 affirmation that you belong to them and they are responsible for you. Have you ever experienced God's personal affection for you? His loving kindness towards you? Parents provide for their children. Offspring inherit from their parents.

God speaks from heaven regarding Jesus after His baptism. In that verse, God publicly makes it known that "this is my beloved Son, in whom I am well-pleased". He lets it be known that He (God) loves Jesus and approves of (smiles on) Him. Oftentimes, a smile of approval from a parent to a child can also serve as evidence of affection.

PARENT'S FAVOR

We know we belong to God because we have His favor. Most of us receive special favor from our parents because of the love and fondness they have for us, as their child. We know we can call upon them in any time of need because of this special love. With God, it is the same. God delights in us. We are the apple of His eye, the center of His favor. He is always thinking about us.

SEALED

According to Eph.1:13, we are sealed, marked, and branded as God's own. The Holy Spirit attests to God's ownership of us. The seal of the Holy Spirit is the assurance that we belong to God. Holy Spirit comes to dwell in us when we accept Christ as our Savior.

OWNING US

God doesn't just own us because He purchased us with His blood, but He also owns us in that He presents proof of our sonship to Him with the giving of the Spirit of adoption (the Holy Spirit).

To admit that something is true is to "own" it. He admits to the truth of our sonship to Him. To admit possession of something or a personal relationship with someone is to "own" them. (**2Chron. 7:14 KJV** "my people") Finally, to "own" is to place an identification mark on as a public sign of ownership. Through the indwelling presence of the Holy Spirit, God has identified us as belonging to Him. We are His people and are called by His name.

29

TRUST AND OBEY

KEEP HIS COMMANDMENTS

According to the Bible, we are to **obey God's law**, His commandments, His Word. Then it says that if we do keep His law, we will have long life and peace. The Bible tells us in Pro.3:5, that we are to trust in the Lord with all of our heart. <u>So, we are to **obey,** and we are to **trus**t in God.</u> To "trust in" means to have "faith in" to rely on. Also, if we trust in the Lord with all of our heart, we will find favor in the sight of God and man. So, God is pleased by our complete trust, or faith in Him.

OWN THINKING

Most of us are somewhat familiar with the passage of scripture in Pro. 3 and have probably even quoted verses 5 and 6 ourselves. We know that it tells us to believe in God for everything, and He will guide us, direct us, and show us what to do, which will ultimately work out for our benefit. So why is it then, that we end up taking a wrong turn or making a wrong choice that causes us hardship and loss? The answer is in the second part of **verse 5 "lean not unto thine own understanding".** <u>We make decisions</u>

based on our own understanding rather than on our reliance on God's leading. Although He is trying to lead us and direct our path, we begin to waiver in our faith and not trust in His ability and in His willingness to help us. All things work together for our good. In other words, we must trust that His intent is always toward our good. We need to die to self, self-reliance and self-centeredness.

WILLINGNESS

"If ye be **willing** and **obedien**t, ye shall eat the good of the land". (**Is. 1:19 KJV**) Being willing means to have the inclination to say "yes" to God, and to follow up with action. In other words, obedience. When we waver in our trust in God, we become unwilling to obey. This blocks out whatever directive He was trying to give us and cancels out any possibility of receiving the grace and blessing that He had in mind for us. We must be willing to trust God for all things and all situations.

TRUST HIS WORD

Another reason we don't obey God is because we don't fully trust God to keep His Word. God **MUST** keep His Word. He swore by his Own Self (because there was none greater than He to swear by) to keep His promises. He hastens His Word to perform it. Hasten means hurries to perform it. "God is not a man that He should lie; neither the son of man, that He should repent: Hath He said, and shall He not do it? Or hath He spoken, and shall He not make it good?" (**Numb.23:19 KJV**) He will not alter the thing that has gone out of His lips.

SELF-DECEPTION

If we believe something, we will act accordingly. For example, if we really believe it is going to rain, we will prepare for it, like close windows or carry an umbrella. Belief and action are linked together. When we are not obedient or compliant with God's Word, it is probably because we don't have full confidence in His promises and His warnings. It is disrespectful to know God's Word, fail to obey it, and think there are no consequences. It is deceiving our own selves. "God is not mocked, whatsoever a man soweth, that shall he also reap." (**Gal.6:7 KJV**)

CONFIRMATION OF TRUST

So, avoid the consequences of disobedience; trust God and obey Him. If we are not obeying, it is because we are lacking somewhere in our trust. When we ask God's guidance for every situation, we are saying that we acknowledge that He is the All-knowing, All-wise God of this universe.

30

JESUS, AUTHOR AND FINISHER OF OUR FAITH

JESUS IS THE AUTHOR

As Christians, the name and person of **Jesus** has become familiar, even too familiar to us. Sometimes we can get so familiar and casual with His name and persona that it becomes a common thing to us, even so far as taking His name in vain sometimes. Persona means how we perceive or see Him.

We need to see Him as more than what He can do for us, but we should see Him as who He is. He is Our Father, Lord and Savior, Holy Spirit, Our God. In Christ is all the fullness of the Godhead in bodily form. He is our progenitor. This means our ancestor from whom we, in the Body of Christ, <u>stem from</u>. We are spiritually His descendants. We are His spiritual bloodline.

THE ORIGINATOR

The Bible says that Jesus is **the author** and **finisher** of our faith. As the author of our faith, He is the **originator** of our faith. Our faith is founded upon Him and His work. He is the cause and the basis for what we believe. Our faith begins with belief in Him. He is responsible for the inspired writings that instruct, reprove, convict and correct us for living this life of faith.

OUR EXAMPLE

Not only is Jesus the author, but He also is our **example**. The first part of **Heb. 12:2 KJV** says "looking unto Jesus", which means looking unto Him as our example of how to live the Christian life. We need to keep our spiritual mind stayed on Him and trust Him for direction. His life defines and exemplifies what living everyday life as a Christian is. His Word is our guide to coping with the circumstances of life.

THE SOURCE OF POWER

Jesus is the **source** of power to live the Christian life in victory, so that we can hear God say at the end, "well done, good and faithful servant." **(Matt. 25:23 KJV) John 15:5** says, "I am the vine, ye are the branches: He that abideth in me, and I in him, the same bringeth forth much fruit: for without me ye can do nothing." In other words, you cannot produce anything useful to God without Him. It is He who enables and equips us to be the servants for Him that will bring Him glory.

He upholds everything by the Word of His power, which means that the power of His Word sustains all things. All of creation which He spoke into being still exists by the power of His Word. He is the **Creator**. He said, Let there be..., and there was, and still remains today. "All things were made by Him; and without Him was not anything made that was made." **(John 1:1-3 KJV)** His Word is manifested by His power.

In **Matt.28:18 KJV**, Jesus says," …all power is given unto me in heaven and earth." He has given to us power over all the power of the enemy, but He is the <u>power</u> <u>source</u>.

THE FINISHER

Col.2:10 KJV says. "And ye are **complete** <u>in</u> <u>Him</u>…" You need nothing more. He appoints the time for our Christian race to end (to finish, to be completed). We are finished when He says we're finished. So, the conclusion of this age (the end times) will be Jesus' return, the abolishment of sin and <u>full salvation</u> for us. Our eternal presence with Jesus is the final reward of our faith. Then there will be no more need for faith. Faith will have come to its end. Then, like the last words that He spoke from the cross, it will be **<u>finished</u>**.

31

GOD CONFIRMS HIS POWER

OMNIPOTENT GOD

We know that our God is omnipotent. This means that He is all-powerful. He has all power in His hands. God desires that our faith not stand in the wisdom of men, but in the power of God. God confirms His power through demonstration.

FOR HIS GLORY

Examples of this are shown all through the Bible. God demonstrates His power not only in the Bible, but also in our everyday lives. These demonstrations are always **for His glory** and for our edification and encouragement.

In **John 11: 25 KJV**, Jesus was teaching Martha and others that "I am the resurrection and the life" as He brought her brother, Lazarus back to life after being dead four days. This demonstration encouraged those who saw it and gave glory to God.

PROTECTION FROM ENEMIES

Rom. 8:31 KJV says, "If God be for us, who can be against us." Our enemies have no chance to win against the power of God. The Bible tells us in Ps.27:2, that the power of God will cause our enemies to stumble and fall. God's power shut the mouths of the ravenous lions, protecting His faithful servant, Daniel, from any harm when he was thrown in with them for praying to his God, and God received the glory.

DON'T COMPROMISE

God wants us to stand firm in our faith, and not yield to the pressures of the world's ways. We are not to compromise on God's Word. He will uphold us with the right hand of His righteousness (His right hand of power). In the book of Daniel, King Nebuchadnezzar had enacted an ordinance that anyone who did not bow down to his image would be put to death in the fiery furnace. Shadrach, Meshach, and Abednego gave a confident answer to the angry King Nebuchadnezzar that their God is able to deliver them from him as well as from the fiery furnace, and that they would not bow.

The next morning after they were thrown into the furnace, the King observed a fourth person (Jesus) in the furnace with them, and they emerged completely unharmed. The King then decreed that all people were to respect their God and could not ever speak against Him. Here, again, God received the glory for the demonstration of His power.

COMMIT YOUR WAY

Ps. 37:5 KJV tells us to "commit thy **way** unto the Lord". **Commit** means to give or entrust for safekeeping. This means to commit our course of life or mode of action Unto the Lord. Let us live our lives based on our dependence on the power of God to lead us and take care of us in every situation. All the promises of God in Christ are yea and amen. We are able to cast all of our cares upon Him for He cares for us. We can boldly seek Him for help. He commands us to be strong and courageous because He is with us. He will never leave nor forsake us.

WHAT ABOUT US TODAY?

How many times has God demonstrated His power in our own lives? The answer is every day. Each day that He lets us open our eyes and start a new day is confirmation of His power. Recall the many times God opened doors for you that no man could close, and how He closed doors that no man could open, and even how He made a way out of no way. "This is the Lord's doing, and it is marvelous in our eyes". (**Matt.21:42 KJV**) All glory be to God!

32

EXERCISE YOUR SENSES

USEFUL EXERCISE

1Tim.4:8 KJV tells us, "For bodily exercise profiteth little, but godliness is profitable unto all things, having promise of the life that now is, and of that which is to come."

We need to exercise daily in God so that our **spiritual senses** become strong, alert and accurate. Living a life that is disciplined in the things of God is more useful than physical appearances. The things of God mentioned here refer to basics: prayer, bible study, meditation, obedience to authority and to God's Word, sharing the gospel, praise and worship, and fellowship with the saints. Exercise means training oneself with a behavior over and over again until it becomes a habit.

WEAK SENSES

If we are not daily doing things that will strengthen our spiritual senses, they become weak, non-functional and useless. We become stagnated in our spiritual growth. We remain shallow and immature, lacking any depth as babes in the Lord.

BECOMING STRONG

As we are faithful to doing the habits that strengthen ourselves in the basic things of God, Holy Spirit can give to us even more in strong meat, which means more revelation and illumination into the mysteries of God and the application of them. Heb. 5:14 talks of becoming of full age, that is mature <u>by reason of use</u> having our senses exercised to discern (or perceive) both good and evil.

DISCERNING

While practicing basic behaviors and listening to the Holy Spirit and obeying His leading, we can become mature in the spiritual ability to <u>discern</u> and distinguish between the utterances of true spirits and false ones. However, **1Cor. 12:11AMP** says, "All these (gifts, achievements, abilities) are inspired and brought to pass by one and the same Holy Spirit, Who apportions to each person individually (exactly) as He chooses." Following His leading gives us opportunities to practice in discerning right from wrong. As we listen and follow Holy Spirit, we become experienced in His ways, and our senses are heightened.

DON'T GET LAZY

When we are enjoying the fellowship of the Holy Spirit and the grace of God, it is important not to take it or Him for granted. It is easy to become lazy and complacent. Stay committed. Remain "steadfast, unmovable always abounding in the work of the Lord, forasmuch as ye know that your labor is not in vain in the Lord." (**1Cor. 15:58 KJV**) Yes, consistent exercise takes effort and dedication, but afterwards there will be a great reward gained that cannot be obtained without it. We will gain the eternal things which are the most valuable, and we will be in the will of God.

BY REASON OF USE

"By reason of use" means by reason of practice and experience. **1John 4:*1* KJV** says, "Beloved, believe not every spirit, but <u>try</u> the spirits whether they are of God; because many false prophets are gone out into the world". Not everyone who talks about God is from God. "Everyone who confesses openly his faith in Jesus Christ (the Son of God, who came as an actual flesh and blood person) comes from God and belongs to God". (**1John 4:2-3 MSG**) Also, We belong to God, and those who know God listen to us. Those who are not from God do not listen to us. This is how we know the Spirit that is true and the spirit that is false. Exercise your spiritual senses and glorify God.

33

RESURRECTIION POWER

THE DEATH OF CHRIST

"For all have sinned and come short of the glory of God". (**Rom. 3:23 KJV**) "For the wages of sin is death; but the gift of God is eternal life through Jesus Christ Our Lord". (**Rom. 6:23 KJV**) "For God so loved the world that He gave His only begotten Son, that whosoever believeth in Him should not perish, but have everlasting life." (**John 3:16 KJV**)

Christ paid the wages of sin (the cost of our sin) for us when He voluntarily sacrificed His own body and blood. If we only believe what He did (died for our sins) and believe who He is (the only begotten Son of God), instead of eternal death (in Hell), we can have eternal life (in the presence of God forever). Christ knew God's plan for our salvation. God is not willing that any should perish), so He prepared a body for Christ to die in our place. Jesus said, "I, Lo, I come (in the volume of the book it is written of me,) to do thy will, O God" (**Heb. 10:7 KJV**) Then Jesus took on our sins and bore them in His own body. After much torture, pain and shame, Jesus hung His head and died, so we wouldn't have to.

WHAT HAPPENED WHEN HE DIED?

There were physical manifestations in the earth when Jesus died. Darkness fell upon the earth for about three hours. The earth shook, and the rocks were split. There were also spiritual manifestations. When Jesus died, the curtain of the temple (that separated us sinful people from our Holy God), was torn in two from top to bottom. Christ's death for our sins gave us access to approach our Holy God. And this, in itself was amazing. But it was not the most amazing thing that happened.

RELEASE OF POWER

The most amazing thing was that Jesus didn't stay dead! After being buried for three days, Jesus arose from the grave. When Jesus arose, He set into motion an eternal chain of events propelled by the extraordinary power which was released with His Resurrection. Graves of saints opened, and many bodies arose. He triumphed over sin and death when He arose from the grave. Prophecy was fulfilled. God's plan was accomplished. Jesus freed us from the dominion of sin and the fear of death. Now, by the power of His resurrection, we shall also rise again, not only in our spiritual bodies, but also in this natural life. His resurrection from death has released resurrected life in every area of our natural lives, if we will yield to Him.

AVAILABLE TO US

The same supernatural power that raised Jesus from the dead is made available to us as believers. Through our faith in Jesus, we have the victory and power over all the power of the enemy. We can triumph over sin in our own lives, but we must first die to sin. His Resurrection gives us power to live for Christ.

EXPERIENCE IT

When we are in Christ, by faith we can experience His Resurrection power. God's Resurrection power is what makes us more than conquerors through Him that loved us. It is what always causes us to triumph in Christ. We now have power over our flesh. Resurrection power will lift up the standard against the enemy that will cause him to retreat. Resurrection power heals, renews, births, produces, restores, refreshes, builds up, promotes, strengthens, increases, advances, encourages, purifies, and proves.

34

THE SEED OF WORSHIP

PLANTING SEED

When we worship God, we are planting seed that will result in a harvest of increase. Plant your seed of worship into the heart of God. We water the seed of worship with our obedience, tears of humility, awe and love for Him. God will receive an acceptable sacrifice of holy, consecrated worship from believers, and God will give the increase. He responds to sincere worship by equipping us, spiritually and naturally. We worship God when our thoughts, words and actions line up with His will.

FRUIT OF THE SEED

The seed of worship will begin to bring forth fruit. Some of that is manifested as <u>growth and maturity of the nine fruit of the Spirit:</u> love, joy peace, longsuffering, gentleness, goodness, faith, meekness and temperance.

MUCH FRUIT

With true worship can come also revelation of an assignment. (**Acts 13:2 KJV**) "As they ministered to the Lord and fasted, the Holy Ghost said, separate me Barnabas and Saul for the work whereunto I have called them".

In Matt.15:22, the Syrophoenician (Greek) woman worshipped Jesus (for she called Him Lord) and received spiritual healing for her daughter who was demon-possessed, although Jesus denied her request at first.

When we acknowledge that He is Lord with reverence, we are worshipping Him. The woman with the issue of blood, believing who He was and that He alone was able to heal her, pressed through the crowd just to touch the hem of His garment and received physical healing. So, spiritual healing and physical healing are available for worshippers.

True worship from us is God's will and releases the power of God to draw people unto Himself. The Samaritan woman acknowledged and spread the word of who Jesus was, and many came to believe in Him. The fruit was that she became a witness for Christ because of her worship. Because she lifted Jesus up (exalted Him), Jesus drew people unto Himself.

Dwelling in a place of worship to God affords us deliverance, protection and peace. These are more fruit of true worship.

There are other fruit (benefits) of worship. The Bible says that we will "bless the Lord", from Whom we receive forgiveness, healing, redemption, loving-kindness, tender mercies, satisfaction of our every need, and strength.

INTIMACY WITH GOD

Another fruit of the seed of worship is a more intimate relationship with God. "God is a Spirit. They that worship Him must worship Him in spirit and in truth". (**John 4:23-24**) **James 4:8 AMP** says to "come close to God, and He will come close to you".

When you genuinely worship God in spirit and in truth (for real), God will meet you in that place of worship. He will begin to love on you and to reveal to you more about who He is and who you are in Him. Your relationship with Him will grow stronger and closer.

INCREASE

There will be increase (fruit) resulting from the seed of true worship. Healing, deliverance, provisions, spiritual growth, (including spiritual gifts), spiritual insight, protection and guidance are manifested.

35

SURRENDER ALL

IDOLATRY

The Bible describes how men forsook the love of God and in ignorance began to worship man-made idols which led them to become morally corrupt. In today's terms –anything that we put before our worship and obedience to God is an idol, and when we do this, we are idolaters.

Are we willing to give up any and everything that we have given preeminence over God? What have we let take God's place, His position as ruler over our lives? What things have become more important than obeying God? What do we need to let go of or give a place of less importance, so God can have His rightful place of highest importance?

SURRENDER ALL

Are we willing to surrender all to God? To surrender means to give up, give in, concede, release, give, forfeit your rights or claim to. These things are not so much natural as they are spiritual things. Correcting things in the spirit first will lead to things in the natural becoming corrected also.

We need to surrender any thoughts, words, or actions that are contrary to God's Word. These things should not govern us. Only God's Word should govern us. The Bible says that who or whatever you yield yourself to (to obey), that is your God. (Ex: your children, your spouse, your job etc.) Refuse to be ruled by lust of the eye, lust of the flesh or the pride of life. **These** spirits are not of the Father but are of the world. Some of these may manifest as: self- pity, doubt, fear, negativity, partying, smoking, gossiping, criticism, selfishness, alcoholism, sexual lust, profanity, laziness, greed, gluttony, not giving money, time, or energy. We need to be super-diligent to guard our heart from evil influences. **Then, "SUBMIT YOURSELVES UNTO GOD; RESIST THE DEVIL AND HE WILL FLEE." (James 4:7 KJV)**

CHARACTERISTICS OF A SURRENDERED LIFE

A person with a surrendered life must be <u>consecrated.</u> The Bible says in Rom.12:1 to present our bodies as an acceptable sacrifice holy unto God. To be consecrated is to live a life that does not yield our members as instruments of unrighteousness, but unto God. The consecrated person should have <u>died to sin</u> and now live a new life completely relying on and trusting in Christ. This person's life should be <u>submitted to God's will,</u> and He should live a life of <u>unquestioning service.</u>

SURRENDER YOUR HOPES, DREAMS, PLANS AND DESIRES

We should be willing to put ours on a backburner and submit instead to God's plans for us, which are the best. "Seek ye first the Kingdom of God and His righteousness, and all these things will be added unto you". **(Matt.6:33 KJV)**

We honor God by making Him the Lord over our lives. That means giving Him preeminence and priority over anything we might devise in our own minds to bring ourselves some sort of satisfaction. We need to change our ways.

We need to surrender even our thought patterns that do not line up with God's will. We need to surrender our relationships that do not line up with God's will. When we make plans without seeking God first, we are not surrendering to Him full control of our lives.

We need to surrender every pet sin that we like to do and don't want to quit doing. God wants it all.

He does not want us to withhold or hold back anything. Let us let go of our idols. God said "thou shall have no other God's before me". **(Ex. 20:3 KJV)**

36

THE PROPHETIC SPIRIT

THE HOLY GHOST

God sent the Holy Ghost to dwell in every believer. The Holy Ghost is the Prophetic Spirit. Prophetic means having to do with prophecy. Prophecy may be defined as a divinely inspired prediction, instruction or exhortation. The Holy Ghost is described as the Comforter (*exhorter*, encourager, helper) which shall teach us all things and bring everything to our remembrance that Jesus has taught us. He is further described as the Spirit of Truth who will guide us into all truth (*instruction*). He will announce and declare to us the things that are to come (*prediction*). Prophecy may be prediction (fore-telling) or proclamation (forth-telling). Through prophecy, we can speak forth and declare the divine will and purposes of God.

Holy Spirit will not speak His own message, but He will tell whatever He hears from the Father. Holy Spirit knows the mind of God. God unveils and reveals hidden things of His divine counsel through the Holy Spirit. If we have the Holy Ghost, we have the Prophetic Spirit. However, this does not mean that we are a prophet.

THE OFFICE OF A PROPHET

We tend to believe that this "speaking forth" can or should only be done by those that are labeled or acknowledged as "prophets". Certainly, there is such a thing as the "office" of a prophet, which is referred to as one of the gifts God gave to the Body of Christ for its perfecting. However, this is not what we are talking about here.

THE WHOLE COUNSEL OF GOD

God wants to give us counsel so we can have wisdom and understanding to know how to navigate and make decisions in this life. He has provided much advice, information, and directions concerning His desires for us in the written Word or "Logos" of God. In addition to that, He speaks specifically to us through the prophetic Word. It is special revelation targeted to personal circumstances that we may face now or have faced or will face. It is called "Rhema". These two ways combine to assure us that we have the "whole" or "full" counsel of God.

HEAR AND OBEY

We, as believers, have shied away from the idea that all of us may operate in the prophetic as the Holy Spirit gives us revelation, This means that often times when Holy Spirit shows us things and tells us things about ourselves, other people or circumstances, we don't speak it or act on it.

THE SPIRIT OF PROPHECY

Holy Spirit can convey or communicate at any time through any believer He chooses concerning a specific revelation He wants them to have and (possibly) share. It is important to let Holy Spirit lead you in how or when you respond to His revelations.

Sometimes He may choose to use someone in a corporate setting where the spirit is high, and the presence of God is particularly strong. It may happen during zealous praise or sincere worship or fervent prayer. Or He could just give you something for someone you are talking to individually. He could also do it when you are alone.

Remember, the spirit of prophecy comes from the Prophetic Spirit, which is the Holy Ghost. He is the Spirit of the Living God. He is omnipotent, omniscient, and omnipresent, and He wants us to know what God freely gives to us.

37

BEING LIKE GOD

THEE GOD

Everyone (since Adam and Eve), secretly, wants to be like God…Not like **a** God, but like **Thee** God, Jehovah, the great I AM, the only true and living God. That is what explains the popularity of magicians, super-heroes and virtual games of war that defeat the bad guys. Some of this desire for supernatural powers is founded in our spiritual affinity for our Maker (as a child would have, who looked up to his parents). However, some of it is simply a lust for <u>power</u> and control over the world, which stems from the devil himself. Every man knows who the true God is because God has shown them by His creation of the world. **God** says that they are without excuse because His invisible nature, His eternal power, His divinity and <u>attributes</u> have been clearly seen.

ATTRIBUTES OF GOD

God's attributes stem out of His abilities. His abilities are "what He does". He moves by His power. He creates. He gives life. He heals and delivers. He rules the universe. He demands obedience and worship. He commands respect and reverence. He knows everything, and He is everywhere present. God has many more abilities that are not listed here. But many would kill, steal and destroy to have even one of them. Some have already done so, such as Napoleon or Hitler.

THE CHARACTER OF GOD

The character of God is the nature of God. This stems from "who He is". The ultimate aim of the Christian life is to be like Christ in character. God is love, truth, peace, joy, justice, mercy, grace, victorious, forgiving, long-suffering, good, gentle, faithful, temperate, meek, yet strong. And again, God is much more than is listed here.

BE VIGILANT

People would rather bow to a man-made idol than to admit the truth and submit to the only true God. Instead, man seeks to copy, counterfeit, imitate, mimic and pretend that something else, someone else or even they themselves are god. This is because of their inner-most spirit of pride. Ever since pride was found in Lucifer and he was thrown out of heaven, he has used the spirit of pride to contaminate and control God's created people, starting with Adam and Eve. In **Isaiah 14:14 KJV**, Lucifer said, "I will be like the Most High". He wanted to be God then, and he still does. From that time on, Satan has done everything he could think of to fool and trick people into worshipping and obeying him. Don't get swallowed up by Satan's traps.

CREATED IN HIS IMAGE

We were created in the image of God. So we had the upper hand or advantage from the beginning. **The Bible** says that we are ambassadors for Christ. In other words, we are to represent Christ and His gospel in this world. We are to BE LIKE CHRIST! We are to exemplify his nature.

True believers don't lust after the abilities of God. They strive, instead, to adopt and exhibit the character of God, which is the nature of God Himself. They do this out of love for God and out of a gratitude for His love for us.

When we became part of Christ, we became partakers of His nature. Through the Holy Spirit living in us, we have the attributes of God. We are directed by the Spirit of the living God. We are born of God and baptized with the Holy Spirit into the Body of Christ. We are like God in this world.

38

MY PEACE

WHAT IS PEACE?

It is more than just quiet. It is also a ceasing of movement, activity, and combative behavior; such as, arguments, fights, strife, discord and noise.

In **Mark 4:39 KJV**, Jesus said to the storm, "Peace, be still, and the wind ceased, and there was a great calm." The wind can be a symbol of torment or trouble, as in "the winds blowing in my life".

STORMS OF LIFE

Don't be afraid when the storms of life come, through tribulation, trials, distress, and frustration. These things are in this world, but you can be confident and certain that God has already conquered these things for you. In Him you can have perfect peace if you keep your mind stayed on Him and because you have confidence in Him.

PEACE IN THE MIDST OF A STORM

We can have peace in the midst of a storm because we can retreat to a place of peace and comfort in God. The Bible says, when we are weak, then are we strong. "...Most gladly therefore will I rather glory in my infirmities, that the power of Christ may rest upon me." (**2Cor. 12:9 AMP**) We are strengthened in that place of power, that place of peace.

FEAR BRINGS TORMENT

"For God so loved the world that He gave His only begotten Son..." (**John 3:16 KJV**) There is no greater love and none more perfect than His. "There is no fear in love, but perfect love casteth out fear: because fear hath torment. He that feareth is not made perfect in love." (**1John 4:18 KJV**) Not that God's love is lacking, it is that he, who is afraid, is lacking in his believing and receiving God's love.

We have learned that fear is not from God. It is from the devil. He uses fear to taunt and torment us in our minds so that we will be worried and afraid. The spirit of fear robs us of our peace.

Let us stop listening to the devil and listen to God instead. God tells us what to think on. He tells us to think on things that are true, honest, just, pure, lovely, of good report, of virtue and of praise.

IN GOD'S WILL

We have peace when we are operating in God's will. When we submit to God's will and are obedient to His will, we will have His peace. Jesus said in **Phil 4:9 KJV**, "**those things** which ye have both learned, and received, and heard, and seen in me, **do**: and the God of peace shall be with you."

MY PEACE

John 14:27 KJV says, "<u>Peace I leave with you</u>, **my peace** I give unto you: not as the world giveth, give I unto you. <u>Let not</u> your heart be troubled, neither let it be afraid."

(**AMP**) "Stop allowing yourselves to be agitated and disturbed; and <u>do not permit yourselves to</u> be fearful and intimidated and cowardly and unsettled"

God has given us His **own** peace. "And the peace of God, which passeth all understanding shall keep your hearts and minds through Christ Jesus" (**Phil. 4:7 KJV**) The world does not understand God's peace because it is spiritually discerned. His peace can keep us through anything that we may be faced with. His peace is not affected or controlled by the circumstances of this physical life. He says for us not to let our heart-peace be disturbed or troubled for we have His peace, and He is the God of peace.

39

WHO DO YOU SAY THAT I AM

WHAT DO PEOPLE SAY?

Jesus is talking to His disciples and asking them what the people of the town were saying about Him. They answered Him that some of the people say that He is John the Baptist, Elijah, Jeremiah or one of the prophets.

Today, some people answer that question saying that He is a force of nature or nature itself, the universe, or our own self-consciousness. Others call Him the Man upstairs, a higher power, an angel, karma, the One who is the Devil's competitor, or the One who sees us from afar.

WHAT THE BIBLE SAYS

In **Matt. 16:16 KJV**, Simon Peters says to Jesus, "Thou art the Christ, the Son of the Living God". In Acts 5:42 AMP, He is Jesus Christ, **the Messiah**, which means in **Ps. 2:2**, the "Anointed One". He's the "King" (**Ps. 24:8 KJV**,), the "Holy Child", "Ruler Over Israel" (**Micah 5:2**), the

"Son of Man" (**Matt. 9:6**), the "Expected One" (**Matt. 11:3**), and the "Son of King David" (**2Sam. 7:12**). He is "the Day Spring" (**Luke 1:78**) He is the "Master" (**Matt. 23:10**), the "Seed of David" (**2Sam. 7:12-16**), the "Root of Jesse" (**Is. 11:1**), "the Christ" (**Acts 17:3**), "God" over all (**Rom. 9:5 AMP**), and much, much more.

WHO DO YOU SAY I AM?

If we have come to personally know God, we may know Him as Savior, Redeemer, Healer, Deliverer, Protector, Warrior, Just King, Righteous One, Sovereign God, Creator, Ruler of the Universe, Lover of our souls, Lifter of our Heads, Miracle Worker. Giver of Life, Bread of Heaven, the Living Word, the Truth and The Life, Lord, and much, much more.

SEEING HIM CLEARLY

Revelation of Who Jesus is comes from the Father. This is what Satan tries to stop us from getting by blinding our minds from the truth. He knows that if we can receive that most important revelation, then we are immediately removed from under his dominion. That revelation opens the door for us to enter into the Kingdom of God.

THE GOSPEL

We must believe and receive the clear knowledge and understanding that Jesus Christ is the Son of the only true and living God, who came to this earth to do good, to suffer and die for our sins; that He was buried, but that God raised Him back to life on the third day; and that He now sits at the right hand of the Father in heaven ever making intercession for us. It is upon this revelation that Christ has built His church, and there is nothing the Devil can do to stop it.

KEYS TO THE KINGDOM

In addition to this, God gives us keys to lock the enemy out of our affairs here on earth. He also gave us keys to unlock the strength and power of heaven to intervene for us and thwart the enemy's attempts. We use the keys to simply declare to be improper and unlawful (bound) on earth what is already not permitted or unlawful in heaven and to declare to be lawful (loosed) on earth what is already loosed in heaven. In other words, the keys are simply bringing things on earth into agreement with how things operate in heaven. Once we speak these keys out of our mouths, the Devil has no defense against them. The Devil recognizes WHO Jesus is. "At the name of Jesus every knee should bow, of things in heaven, and things in earth and things under the earth; and that every tongue should confess that Jesus Christ is Lord, to the glory of God the Father." (**Phil. 2:10-11 KJV**)

40

WALKING IN THE LIGHT OF THE WORD

JESUS IS THE LIGHT

Jesus is the Light of the world according to **John 8:12 KJV.**

It also says "he that followeth me shall not walk in darkness but shall have the light of life". Jesus is the Word. (John 1:1, 14 AMP) So then, the Word is the light of life. The light of the world is the life of the Word. Jesus, the Word, is our life. He called us out of darkness (worldliness) into His marvelous light of life and truth. Jesus is the light that gives light (eternal life) to everyone who will believe on Him.

THE LIGHT OF THE WORD

Walking in the light of the Word means living day to day in the world being guided, not by the world's system of doing things, but by God's way of doing things. It is being guided by God's way of being righteous, which is being guided by His Word. Walking in the light of the Word means living in the safety, the presence, the Spirit, the wisdom and the light of Jesus.

SAFETY OF THE WORD

Walking in the safety of the Word means being guided by the light that the Word shines on our path. The light shows us what is the truth or reality of our circumstances. In the light of God's Word, we will see spiritually everything that He wants to show us (seen and unseen). These things are hidden to the unbeliever who walks in darkness.

PRESENCE OF THE WORD

The presence of God's Word is always as near as our confession of our faith from our own lips and our heart's belief that it is true. Refuse to allow any words from your mouth that are contrary to your faith in His Word, which represents all that He is. His presence is in our prayers of praise and worship for He inhabits the praises of His people. His presence is in His Word that we speak, hear, and read, for He is His Word.

SPIRIT OF THE WORD

The Bible says that the Spirit gives life. The Words of Jesus are activated by the Spirit of Jesus, which is the Holy Spirit. Just as is demonstrated in Gen. 1:2-3 where the Spirit of God moved, and then God spoke creation into being. It is the Spirit that activates the Word of God, so that Word is manifested.

WISDOM OF THE WORD

"Wisdom is the principle thing..." (**Pro. 4:7 KJV**) Knowing the Word of God is able to make us wise unto salvation through faith, which is in

Christ Jesus. Out of the Word of God comes godly wisdom, knowledge and understanding.

And in all thy getting, get understanding, discernment, comprehension, and interpretation.

JESUS IS THE WORD

From the beginning, Jesus was with God, and Jesus (the Word) was God. "God is light, and in Him is no darkness at all". (**I John 1:5 KJV**) God includes Jesus and the Holy Ghost. The light of His Word brings the kind of illumination and spiritual clarity that can only come from a place where there is a total absence of darkness, which is Our God.

41

A SOUND MIND

GUARD YOUR MIND

God has not given us fretful, confused or disturbed minds. God has given us peace that passes all understanding. Yet still some of us find ourselves at times trapped in these conditions. **2Tim.1:7 KJV** says, "For God hath not given us the spirit of fear, but of power, and of love, and a sound mind."

We have power over how we think and what thoughts we let control us. Our thoughts control our actions. "As a man thinketh in his heart, so is he." (**Pro. 23:7 KJV**) We can choose to be controlled by the Devil or by the Word of God. What thoughts are we letting into our hearts? We have to be very diligent about guarding the gateways into our hearts. These gateways are our five senses. The Bible warns us to not give any place to the Devil. Any thought that is against God's Word should be cut down, locked out, and rejected. These negative thoughts are sent by the Devil to keep us under his control or bondage.

RESPOND LIKE JESUS

Three times the Devil tried to tempt Jesus in the wilderness. Each time Jesus used the Word of God to defeat him. We can use that same method to submit to God (His Word), resist the Devil, and He will flee from us. We can use our faith in the power of God's Word to demolish and destroy Satan's negative thoughts and replace them with what lines up with the Word of God.

BELIEVE AND SPEAK

- According to **Job 22:28 KJV**, we can "decree a thing and it shall be established." Speak:
- I have the peace of God.
- The joy of the Lord is my strength.
- I apply the blood of Jesus to my mind, will and emotions.
- I have the mind of Christ.
- I belong to God.

DECREE YOUR DELIVERANCE

Devil, you do not control my mind. You don't tell me what to think or how to feel…because I reject your thoughts and I allow the mind of Christ to dwell in me.

I am free from your yoke of bondage, and I will not allow myself to become entangled again in your mess. I stand strong in my freedom.

I am not confused because confusion is not from God. I control my mind with the thoughts that God wants me to think. I think on things that are worthy of praise and honor and respect and that line up with God's Word. I fill my mind with positive thoughts, not negative.

BE SELF-DISCIPLINED

The Word of God gives me confidence and strength. I am not afraid of the Devil's attempts to steal my joy. My judgment is sound, based on my faith in the Word of God. I discipline my mind and I am calm and well-balanced. I am fully equipped to overthrow the Devil's weapons. He has already been defeated when Jesus spoiled principalities and powers and led captivity captive. The Word of God that I speak by faith will completely shut Satan down, bring him into submission, and cause him to flee from me.

42

IN THE BELOVED

IN LOVE WITH US

By the divine will, the purpose and the choice of God we, the saints, are the consecrated and set apart recipients for His divine agape love. He has chosen us with unmerited favor to receive His peace, which is wholeness, prosperity, quietness and rest. If we are not walking in these things, we are not walking in His will for us. God, our Father, and Jesus, His Son are in love with us. "For God so loved the world that He gave His only begotten Son, that whosoever believeth in Him should not perish, but have ever lasting life." (**John 3:16 KJV**)

PREPARED BY GOD

Because of His love for us, He has blessed us in Christ with every blessing given by the Holy Spirit in the heavenly realm. Just as a parent might do for his child. He makes sure his child is prepared for whatever he/she may encounter once they walk out of their door. After we have accepted Christ as our Savior, we have to now navigate through this world of unbelievers. God has planned ahead for our success.

He clothed us properly for the weather (the circumstances and trials of life). He <u>packed our bags</u> carefully with everything we would need so that we might be prepared as we travel through this life until we reach our heavenly destination.

IN THE BAG

First and foremost, He gave us Jesus, His only Son, to redeem us from our sins. Then He gave us His written and spoken Word to guide us and to lock down the enemy's attempts to steal, kill and destroy us. God gave us His blood (by shedding it on the cross), which has the power to cleanse us from all sin. Also, God gave us the keys to the Kingdom to bind what is unlawful in heaven and to loose what is lawful in heaven. This gives us to know that we don't have to allow the enemy to run havoc in our lives. We have some control over how much we allow him to do. Finally, God gave us the authority and the power of the Name of Jesus to bring everything into submission to His will.

FOR OUR GOOD

God's intention for us is always good. He is the center of our joy, but we are the apple of His eye. We have His full attention, and He should have ours. His thoughts of us are only for our peace and welfare. God loves us so much that before the foundation of the world, He picked us out to be adopted as His own children through Jesus Christ because it pleased Him and was His kind intent for us. Because of this, He shall receive our praise.

IN THE BELOVED

We are in the beloved, that special favored group that God planned for. God yearns for a close relationship with us. We are the objects of His love. So we love Him back. So much wisdom and understanding God has bestowed on us through the sharing of His mysteries with us. The intimacy of a parent sharing his goals and purposes with his child is the relationship we have with God.

We were created. We were planned for. We were sacrificed for. We were adopted. We are sealed and accepted in the beloved. "We are His people and the sheep of His pasture". (**Ps. 100:3 KJV**) He made us to be His own beloved people. God loves us, and His love does not end.

43

ALPHA AND OMEGA

SELF-EXISTING

"I Am Alpha and Omega, the beginning and the ending, saith the Lord, which **is,** and which **was**, and which **is to come**, the Almighty." (**Rev. 1:8 KJV**) Not only does God exist today, but He has always existed before the world began, and will continue to exist in the eternal future. He was from the beginning, is now, and is in the end. Everything is in His presence and under His control. He is Jehovah Shammah, the Lord is there. He is, has been and will always be very present. He was not created but **is the creator** of everything. He Himself is El Shaddai, the Almighty self-sufficient and self-existing. He is the Almighty. Past, present and future are in His hands. God made this world, and without Him was not anything made that was made. In other words, the pottery could not exist before its maker. God fashioned the world with His Words, and it will be by His Words that He brings it to an end.

ALPHA

God is Alpha. Alpha means "the beginning". The beginning means that He is the initiator, the starter, the inception, the origin, the root of the world and all that is in it. God was first before the foundations of the world were laid. In the beginning, God… Creation began in Him and came from Him. God has appointed Christ the heir of all things, through whom also He made the worlds, and Christ upholds all things by the word of His power. We are completely subject to the mercy and love of God. It is His will and purposes that will be carried out regardless of what we do or who we are because His will has preeminence. He is Alpha. That is first in order and highest in importance. He is the potter and we are the clay. We are the work of His hands. He determines when, where, and how we will enter this life, and He also determines when, where and how we will leave it. This is true for us individually as well as for the world in its entirety. However, when the time comes, He will still be God Almighty and in charge. It could be that He will choose to start all over and make us again another. According to Revelation, He will take us, who have been faithful, to live with Him in the new Jerusalem forevermore.

OMEGA

God the Father, Son, and Holy Spirit are constant throughout the ages, from before the beginning of the world to after the end of the world. God is Omega, the last, the ending of everything. Our completion is in Him. He is the culmination of all things. The final stage of all things is in Him. The end of our present existence is in Him. "In Him we live, move and have our being". (**Acts 17:28 KJV**) Outside of Him, we can do none of those things. It is amazing that although everything seems to have taken its own course in life, it all must ultimately come back and be subject to His power and authority. All will come under His judgement and must answer to Him for their deeds. And then, He shall assign to each one rewards or consequences as He sees fit. But everyone will confess that it is Him that we are subject to. It was God at the beginning, and it will be God at the end. God is Omega, the conclusion of a state of being; the conclusion of the prophetic purpose to which He has aimed all along.

44

A RELATIONSHIP WITH JESUS

QUESTIONS

How many of us are saved?

How many are born again?

How many have a relationship with Jesus?

Many will answer the first question by saying, "I am saved because I believe in the birth, death, burial and resurrection of Jesus. Jesus is my Savior." To the second question they might answer, "I've been born of the Spirit. I am a new creature. I've been born again." However, regarding the third question, many might be puzzled as to what is the meaning of the question.

RELATIONSHIP

"What is meant by a relationship with Jesus?" A relationship can be defined as a **connection, an association, or an involvement.** With this definition, a person might say, "Yes, I have a relationship with Jesus. We are <u>connected</u> because He is my God, and I am His child". That connection is like the relationship between family members.

Someone else might say, "Yes, I have a relationship with Jesus because I am <u>associated</u> with Him. We have things in common—common meeting places, our churches. We have common guidelines, the Bible, and we have common associates, other Christians. This association is like what is shared by co-workers on a job. There is rarely any time spent together outside of the job.

INVOLVEMENT

The last definition for relationship has to do with <u>involvement</u>. This is: to engage or employ, to entangle; to influence; envelop or surround. To **engage** is <u>to occupy the attention of a person</u>. An example of this is to engage in conversation.

To **employ** is <u>to enlist someone or something for a purpose.</u> An example is to use the services of or request time and energies of someone to accomplish a goal.

To **entangle** is <u>when two or more things are so mixed in and encompassed with each other that the divisions between the two cannot be seen.</u> An example is strands of a rope or hair can be entangled.

Envelop <u>means to enclose, to surround, to enfold.</u>

AN OUTWARD RELATIONSHIP

How would you describe your relationship with Jesus? Which of the above definitions would apply to you? Are you connected with Jesus? Are you associated with Him?

There is an outward relationship and an inward relationship we can have with Jesus. The outward kind, unfortunately, is the kind that many of us, at some time, have had in our Christian lives. Everything was pretty much on the surface and for "show" only. We went to church just to satisfy our consciences, left there, and went about doing our own thing. There was **no change** in our lives because we were **not influenced** by the Holy Spirit or the preached Word that we did hear. We did not let Holy Spirit or the Word of God occupy our attention. We did not devote time and energy to developing a relationship with Jesus. Also, we had no rapport with God… no times of private conversations based on mutual trust. We didn't love God, neither did we worship Him in Spirit and in truth.

AN INWARD RELATIONSHIP

We must purpose in our hearts to develop an intimate personal relationship with Jesus. We should press to BECOME intricately INVOLVED with Him, continually <u>devoting time and energy</u> to seek His will for every decision, in order to accomplish His purposes. Through the blood of Jesus, we are brought into <u>a right relationship</u> with God. That relationship is one of being acquitted of sin and made righteous. (justified). Now we can come into His presence. The door is open. The way is made for continuous communication between us and God. This is the kind of relationship that we can and should have with Jesus. We need to be so sensitive to His Word and His Holy Spirit, that He guides us through each day. We need to care when we displease or grieve Him by our disobedience. If we love Him, we should care! It should matter to us.

He should have an effect on us. When He is happy, we should be happy. When He is angry, we should be angry. We should love what He loves and hate what He hates. We'll come to know what these things are as we <u>spend time</u> with God and His Word. We need to fully <u>entangle</u> ourselves, let Jesus <u>envelop</u> and surround us from the inside out, and let Him <u>be involved in</u> every aspect of our lives; for then, **He will be our Lord**

45

WHAT'S IN YOUR HAND?

GREATER IS HE

God is able to make use out of what we have already available to us to meet the needs in our lives. God "is able to do exceeding abundantly above all that we ask or think according to the power that worketh in us." (**Eph. 3:20 KJV**) God can make <u>more than enough</u> from what looks like not enough. He is El-Shaddai. God can heal us even when the symptoms don't seem to go away. God can turn the negative attitude of others to our favor if we please Him. He can make even our enemies to be at peace with us. "Greater is He that is in us than he that is in the world." (**1John 4:4 KJV**) God's power is not limited by the world's expectations. Jesus has overcome the world. This means He has conquered it. It is in subjection to Him. Our confidence must be in God.

STAND YOUR GROUND

Moses tells God of his inability to obey Him because the people won't believe God sent him. God asked Moses, "What is that in thine hand?" Moses answers, "a rod". God told him to throw it on the ground. Moses threw it down, and it became a snake. Then Moses ran from it. His response to God's miracle was fear. We must not be afraid to embrace whatever God presents to us, whether it is an opportunity or what seems like a loss. We must trust God implicitly. Our response to Him should always be "Yes Lord" in faith. We do not need to be afraid when God is moving; His doings should always be marvelous in our eyes. "Stand still and see the salvation of the Lord." (**Ex. 14:13 KJV**)

IN YOUR HAND

What is in your hand that God wants to use? Oftentimes we can have the solution to a problem, but just don't see it because we are looking through the eyes of tradition and worldliness. We must allow God to show us another perspective, another way of seeing present circumstances. What has God already provided that we are ignoring or taking for granted? What things? What finances? What gifts? What talents or abilities? What passions, skills, time, or relationships could we have utilized differently?

USE WHAT YOU HAVE

In Luke 19:13, a nobleman went away for a while. Before he left, he gave ten of his servants ten talents (of money) each and told them to "occupy" (or use these) until I return. God is telling us to "use these" resources that you already possess or have access to. Make a change. Look at them like He sees them. Operate out of the norm. Operate from a position of power, not of defeat. Take another look at things, at people, at how you spend your time, how you spend your money. You will be surprised at how even a little change can make a big difference. When we trust God, and obey His Word, He is able to accomplish many things that we never thought of. All things become submissive to God's will as He conforms them for His purposes in our lives. God can "make all grace abound towards us, that we, always having sufficiency in all things, may abound to every good work." (**2Cor. 9:8 KJV**) In Exodus 4:10, Moses told God that he could not speak to Pharaoh and the Israelites as God told him to because he (Moses) was not an eloquent speaker. He said he was "slow of speech and of a slow tongue." Aren't we glad that our victories aren't dependent upon our inadequacies? God told Moses, it is I who made your mouth and your tongue. Take what you have. Make it available for God's use. Thank God for it and trust Him to use it for our victory and for His glory. Let God <u>repurpose</u> it to accomplish what we need and what is His will. What's in **your** hand?

46

THE COMMANDMENT
TO PRAY

WHY PRAY?

Over and over again in God's Word, He commands us to pray. This is how we are to get our needs met and have peace. It is not a suggestion, neither is it a request. We are commanded to pray. Why is it that God makes this command upon us? He commands us to pray because He knows what benefits prayer will bring to us. **Heb. 4:16 KJV** tells us to "come boldly to the throne of grace that we may obtain mercy and find grace to help in the time of need". So obviously, we pray to have mercy, grace and help. To come boldly means without fear or hesitation. Prayer is a form of worship, and God is pleased by it. Our prayers go up to God with incense as a fragrant aroma.

Failure to pray is a failure of duty and service and hinders spiritual progress. It is only by prayer that God can help people. God's great movements in our lives and in the world have been the fruit of prayer. Prayer is absolutely necessary if we want to carry out God's purpose and plan for saving sinners. "Ye have not because ye ask not". (**James 4:2 KJV**) Seek the Lord in prayer for direction in your everyday circumstances.

WHEN AND WHERE

There is no set time or place to pray. Prayer is <u>always</u> appropriate. The manner we pray may be adjusted according to circumstances. We may pray for a long time or for a short time. We may pray in our native language or in the Spirit (unknown tongues). Praying in the Spirit builds us up in our faith. We can pray privately, or we can pray publicly. The main thing is to remember to <u>always</u> pray.

HOW

How should we pray to produce a result? **James 5:16 KJV** says "…the effectual fervent prayer of a righteous man availeth much." The first thing to remember is to rely on the power of the Holy Ghost to give us what and how we ought to pray. With the <u>help of the Holy Ghost</u>, we can pray fervently (with power) and strategically to bring about the change we are praying for. Our prayers are most effective when we **have a sincere heartfelt burden** for a need to be met. We are to pray not only for <u>ourselves</u>, but also for <u>one another</u>.

Our **strategy** when we pray is to be specific in our requests. Pray in faith, believing you receive the answer. Stay focused. Pray according to the Word of God. Pray to the Father in the name of Jesus. Always remember to thank God.

WHAT

There are different kinds of prayer. There is a <u>prayer of faith</u>. You pray this one primarily for yourself. The <u>prayer of supplication</u> is to get the needs of others met. Then there is the <u>prayer of praise and worship</u>, ministering to the Lord. Also there is <u>corporate or united prayer</u>. Believers can usher in the glory of God as they join together in corporate or united prayer and praise.

There is <u>intercessory prayer</u>, where we are standing in the gap in prayer on behalf of another, oftentimes for the unsaved. In the <u>prayer of agreement</u> between two people, Jesus is right there to seal its outcome. Finally, there is <u>warfare prayer</u>. Though we live in the flesh, we war in the spirit against the devil, our enemy, who walks about seeking who he may devour. Using the mighty spiritual armor and weapons of God, we fight against the devil and win. Remember, our victory is only a prayer away.

47

ARE YOU ALL RIGHT WITH GOD?

NOT GOOD ENOUGH

There is none good but one, that is, God. If you would enter into eternal Life, you must continually keep the commandments. None of us qualify for or are deserving of God's love and approval based on our own merit. Trying to keep the commandments of God (His Word) is an on-going work that will continue for the rest of our lives. **Rom.3:23 KJV** says, "All have sinned and come short of the glory of God." It doesn't matter how long we've been saved or how long our family members have been saved or in church. We, personally, must be doers of God's Word daily.

CHECK YOURSELF

We have to answer to God for ourselves. The seeming righteousness of others is in no way imputed to us. We become the righteousness of God in Christ Jesus by accepting His sacrificial act of dying on the cross for us and by obeying His Word. Each day, we must evaluate our choices (give ourselves a spiritual check-up) to see if we are in agreement with God's Word. We are individually accountable to God for how we live our lives.

What is your current status with God? Continuous self-evaluation should leave us little or no time to worry about the tiny specks in the eyes (imperfections) of others. We have to daily stay aware of what **we do, say or think**. Is it pleasing to God? We must take care not to disappoint or shame Him, for we are His examples in this world. When we fall or fail, we have to ask forgiveness and repent so that we can once again align ourselves with His Word. We want to always do what will honor God, making Him our priority.

GOOD STANDING

By Christ taking on the punishment for our sins, we have been placed in a right relationship with Him. All is well between us and Jesus. We are forgiven, and our sins have been taken away. We remain in this "good standing" state until we transgress (be disobedient) again.

It is true that Christ's blood sacrifice has atoned for all of our sins—past, present and future. However, He tells us that we are to walk (live) in holiness. That is, walk in a way that reflects our relationship with The Holy One, Jesus Christ.

GOD IS FAITHFUL

God will never remove His love from us. God says that He has loved us with an everlasting love. Just as we can love our children and still be at odds with them over their behavior, we can be at odds (not in agreement) with our loving heavenly Father when we disobey Him; in other words, when we sin with our thoughts, actions or feelings. Continuous self-reflection is needed to monitor the state of our relationship at any given moment. We don't want anything to hinder our fellowshipping with Christ. Holy Spirit can help us. He can show us our unrepented sins so we can repent and be restored to the refreshing in the presence of the Lord.

GETTING WEIGHED

When the scales of our life are weighed, we don't want to be found wanting, or lacking in our determination to obey God. We want His approval every day. We don't want to offend Him with disobedience. Therefore, let us live every day in continual repentance, not for yesterday's transgressions or tomorrow's, but for today's. Each day has enough challenges of its own to be accountable for.

48

THE SPIRIT OF LOVE

GOD IS LOVE

The spirit of love is God's kind of love. It is agape, unconditional. God has given us that spirit. "For God is love". (**1John 4:8 KJV**) This love that comes from God is a kindly feeling and a benevolent intent for us. His intent is always for our good. The spirit of love is what we have toward God, our Creator. It is our reverent devotion towards Him. The spirit of love is also the kindly affection we **should** have towards one another.

LOVE IS COMPASSIONATE

"His compassions fail not". (**Lam. 3:22 KJV**) The spirit of love is a caring spirit. It is a giving spirit. It is an unselfish spirit that puts the concerns of others before its own. 1John 4:20 says that anyone who hates his brother (brethren) does not love God. We experience and understand God's love through Christ's sacrificial death. The world will experience God's love through the way we treat them. If you see a brother or sister in need and have the means to do something about it but do nothing, you will leave that person asking, "where is God's love in you?" God's love should be shown in deeds through us.

FROM GOD

The spirit of love is one of the fruit of the Holy Spirit. So then, the spirit of love is the result of the presence of the Holy Spirit within us. God has given us the spirit of love through the Holy Ghost. In **John 14:16 (AMP)**, Jesus says, "And I will pray the Father, and He shall give you another Comforter, that He may abide with you forever." The spirit of love always seeks to care for, fight for, protect and provide for God's people.

LOVE, NOT FEAR

Contrary to the spirit of love is the spirit of fear. The spirit of fear is not from God. It is from the devil. It works against God's purposes. Instead of giving benevolence, it seeks to torment, condemn and intimidate people and cause them to be paralyzed as far as doing the will of God. If we know that we are walking in the Spirit of God's love, we don't have to be afraid because we know that His love is protecting and taking care of us.

IN OPERATION

When the spirit of love is operating, it is demonstrated in particular ways. The spirit of love draws people unto itself. It does not repel. It covers their weaknesses. It does not expose. It sees the good in a person. It does not find faults. It esteems others better than themselves. It is positive, not negative. It includes, not excludes. It looks out for the interests of others. The spirit of love is empathetic; that is, understanding and sensitive to the feelings of others. It anticipates the needs of others. It is supportive and encouraging. It is always hopeful, does not waver, is not jealous, is trusting and forgiving. It is always helpful and concerned. It shares resources including time and can relate to some common experiences.

WITHOUT LOVE

Only what we do out of love has any value to God at all. No matter what acts of kindness we may perform, God does not approve or applaud them if done without love. Remember that God is love. Operating without love is operating without God. **John 13:35 KJV** says, "By this shall all men know that ye are my disciples, if ye have love for one another." "...God's love has been abundantly poured out within our hearts through the Holy Spirit who was given to us." Now let us generously pour it out to others.

49

INORDINATE AFFECTATION

WHAT IS RIGHT

The Word of God is the standard of righteousness or what is right for every person created in His image. However, some do not adhere to or abide by it. Some refuse to be directed or corrected by any standard of order. They would rather yield their mind and body to thoughts and behaviors that are contrary to God's Word. These behaviors are unacceptable and spiritually unlawful; in other words, sin.

DOMINION

Rom. 6:12-14 AMP admonishes us, as believers, to no longer let sin reign or have dominion over our physical bodies, obeying its lusts and passions. Instead, we need to offer our members (our bodies) as instruments of righteousness (God's way of being right). We can exert authority over our bodies and thoughts, bringing them into subjection, making them a slave to us. Because of God's grace, we are no longer slaves to sin. So, sin no longer has dominion or control over us.

WORKS OF THE FLESH

The world wants to live by an "anything goes" way of thinking. "I can do anything with anybody, and there is nothing wrong with it". But God's Word says, "Woe unto them that call evil good and good evil". (**Is. 5:29 KJV**)

The world's idea of sexual relationships is **inordinate**. This means it is secular, unregulated, devilish, selfish and rebellious. "… The practices of the sinful nature (of man) are clearly evident: they are sexual immorality, impurity, sensuality (total irresponsibility, and lack of self-control)". (**Gal. 5:19 AMP**)

WHAT THE WORD SAYS

Those that say it's ok to have "eros" (sexual desire) for the same gender are absolutely contradicting God's Word. In Rom. 1:26, the Bible calls **Lesbianism** "vile" affection. Vile means abominably wicked; shameful or evil. Rom. 1:27 says that men who pursue other men (**Homosexuals**) will receive the just penalty for their wrongdoing.

THE 6TH DAY

On the 6th day of creation, God created male and female and told them to be fruitful and multiply. The concept of two women or two men being sexual mates is absurd (nonsensical), because the underlying purpose of opposite genders is for procreation. **1Cor. 11:9 KJV** says "…the woman was created for the man". God saw what He created and said it was very good. God sealed and validated that everything He made was good and proper. Who is it that will reject the counsel (purpose, will) of God?

NOT GOD'S PLAN

Any perverted or evil longings in our flesh are to be put to death before they destroy us. This includes adultery, fornication, masturbation, all uncleanness and inordinate behaviors. This is a kind of idolatry because it replaces our devotion to God. "They that do such things shall not inherit the Kingdom of God." (**Gal. 5:20-21 KJV**)

We should purpose daily to protect our bodies, souls and spirits from anything that will feed any such longings. We can keep ourselves from contamination with the power of the Holy Ghost and self-discipline. As Christians, we know that the Bible is right, without any ifs, ands or buts. We must take a strong stand against anything that is contrary to it—including inordinate affection, which opposes the very purposes for which God made us.

50

ISSUES OF THE HEART

BE CAREFUL

Pro. 4:23 EXB says "Be careful what you think." Above all guard your heart. Protect your heart because your life flows from what's in your heart. This is saying that the life we are living is the direct result of the "thoughts and intents" of our hearts.

FROM HEART TO MOUTH

"Good people bring good things out of the good they stored (treasured) in their hearts. But evil people bring evil things out of the evil they stored (treasured) in their hearts. For the mouth speaks what overflows from the heart." (**Luke 6:45 EXB**)

SELF-DECEPTION

What is it that we have stored (treasured) down in our hearts? We treasure it, so we hide and protect it from exposure. We think this hidden treasure gives us a kind of power to deceive other people. However, we are only deceiving ourselves. These **heart** problems (**issues**) are not hidden at all. They expose themselves for all to hear every time we open our mouths. "For out of the abundance (many thoughts) of the heart, the mouth speaks". (**Luke 6:45 AMP**)

OUT OF ORDER

Let us examine our own hearts to see what evil thoughts or feelings we are harboring (hiding). According to **James 3:16 EXB**, "where jealousy or envy and selfish ambition are, there will be confusion, chaos, disorder and every kind of evil practice". When we consider our own hearts, what kind of evil thoughts do we find that could account for the confusion and disorder in our lives?

STORED UP EVIL

Is there <u>jealousy</u> or <u>envy</u> over someone else's gift or blessing? Can we identify <u>slothfulness</u> or <u>laziness</u> that can account for habitual tardiness? Are we <u>stubborn</u> at times when it comes to complying with certain requests from authority figures? Do we feel that the rules apply to everyone but us because of <u>pride</u>?

Do we feel that we are <u>always</u> <u>right</u> and everyone else is wrong? Are there some people that we have a <u>grudge</u> against or that we just don't like? Do we tend to make wrong assumptions (<u>judgements</u>) about people? Do we feel unwelcomed or unappreciated by others? Are we easily hurt or <u>offended</u>? Does <u>procrastination</u> cause consequences that make ours and others' lives more difficult? Is the <u>anger</u> we have in our hearts always somebody else's fault? These are the evil **issues of the heart** that work <u>strife</u> and <u>confusion</u> and every <u>evil</u> <u>work</u> in our lives.

GET YOUR HEART IN ORDER

Phil. 2:3 KJV says, "Let nothing be done through strife or vainglory, but in lowliness of mind let each esteem other better than themselves." In the Amplified it says, "Do nothing from selfishness or empty conceit, but with an attitude of humility [being neither arrogant nor self-righteous], regard others as more important than yourselves."

James 3:18 AMP tells us to sow seeds of peace in order to reap righteousness. "The seed whose fruit is righteousness (spiritual maturity) is sown (planted, started) in peace (good will) by those who make peace."

We need to repent and ask God for help. "Create in me a clean heart, O God; and renew a right spirit within me." (**Ps. 51:10 KJV**)

51

IT'S ALL GOD

THE PLAN OF GOD

From Genesis to Revelation, God is the Author and Finisher of our faith. He is the Creator and planner of the universe. His eyes search the earth for those whose heart is committed to Him to strengthen them. His sovereignty prevails overall, causing, allowing or prohibiting what occurs. He uses every occurrence as part of His tightly woven fabric (plan) of purpose.

GOD ANSWERS PRAYERS

In many scriptures in the Bible, God tells us that He loves us and that all things will work out for the good of them that love Him and are the called according to His purpose. Many instances are sighted where He hears and answers the prayers of His people. So, when we pray, we must not be discouraged, confused or doubtful. We must be convinced that what we believe God for, He is doing.

CONFIDENCE IN GOD

In the present moment, we may not see the results manifested yet. But we must know that what we see is part of the process. God still is in control. He really does have all the world in His hands. As the righteous, we may pray fervently and according to God's will and not yet see much being availed at that moment. But we have to be confident that God has heard us, and therefore, we expect to have the petitions that we desired of Him.

MANIFESTATIONS BY GOD

And when the manifestations come, let us not become boastful or prideful and forget that it is God who brought us out into a better place. After we pray, we must wait patiently on the Lord, staying strong in faith, and remembering it will manifest in His perfect timing. We should expect the unexpected. So, while we are waiting for God to answer our prayers, solve our problems and the world's problems, we must <u>trust</u> <u>and</u> <u>believe</u>, for no one can understand the greatness of His wisdom. His thoughts are higher than ours. It's not about our money, strength, intelligence, skills or cleverness that brings us the victory. All of these abilities are given to us by God. We must purpose in ourselves to never take glory for our successes. All of the glory belongs to God.

SECURE IN GOD

We may not understand God's plan, but we must remain steadfast. We must just continue doing good as much as we know to do. We must continue delighting ourselves in the Lord (enjoying serving Him). Let us commit our ways (depend on, rely on) unto the Lord, and know that He will take care of us. We can rest in this knowledge.

ONLY GOD

Without God we can do nothing. He is our Provider. He is our Healer. He is our Battle-fighter. It is the Lord who sanctifies us. It is the Lord who saved and redeemed us. It is God who gives us the victory through our Lord Jesus Christ. He is Jehovah Shammah, everywhere present. No flesh can ever have His glory. Even our very existence is **not about us, it is about Him** and His will being done. "By Him therefore, let us offer the sacrifice of praise to God continually, that is, the fruit of our lips giving thanks to His name." (**Heb. 13:15 KJV**) God the Father, God the Son, and God the Holy Ghost, **It's All God**! It's His doing and His business, and it is marvelous in our eyes.

52

GOD IN CONCERT

WORKING TOGETHER

The dictionary defines "in concert" as: in agreement, in conjunction (working) with, two or more people or things doing something or are involved in something. The Father, Son and Holy Ghost, the three persons of Our God, rule in concert. They do everything as one. They co-exist and cooperate together.

ONE GOD

Deut. 6:4 KJV tells us that "the Lord Our God is One Lord." "In the beginning was the Word (**Jesus**), and <u>the Word was **with God**</u> and <u>the Word **was God**</u>." (**John 1:1-2**) "And the **Spirit** <u>of God</u> moved on the face of the waters." (**Gen. 1:2**) All three were working together to accomplish creation of our world. They are inseparable, and they exist as One God.

SAME ESSENCE

They are one in essence. The essence of something is the basic nature of it, the properties of it. The essence of our God is <u>goodness, truth, love,</u> <u>power</u> and <u>holiness</u>. They are <u>love</u> manifested. Together as one, they have all <u>power</u>. They are one in <u>holiness</u> because the Father is holy. Jesus, the Son, is holy. The Spirit is holy.

ONE DEITY

Gen. 1:26 shows that God is more than one person. In that verse He says, "Let **us** make man in **our** image, after **our** likeness…" Here He identifies Himself as **Elohim**, a plural God, and as the only true God who is worthy to be worshipped. Father, Son and Holy Ghost, they are the Trinity, the three persons that are one God. They carry out one plan for one purpose. As one deity, they accomplish everything in accord with the counsel of one will.

For example, when someone touches your arm, you say, "they touched me". They <u>touched your person</u>, which is **you.** Even though your arm is a specific part, they are still touching you. God the Father, God the Son, and God the Holy Ghost is each one specific, but are, all together, still God.

IN HARMONY

The harmony (singleness) of the three persons of God is unique from any other gods or idols worshipped by man. The three of them are not in competition for the praises of man. Neither is one higher or greater than the other. They testify of one another's deity. When we worship, we worship all three, for there is no separation of them.

Not only are they working together in concert, but they are also doing it in harmony, each as an enhancement to the others for the perfect end result. They are so uniquely tuned in to one another, that the result is a harmony that could not be otherwise achieved. As an orchestra is synchronized to produce one melodious symphony of music, so is our God synchronized to produce the events of our lives. God's work is excellent, mighty, purposeful and continuous. Our God is great! There is **none** like Him.

Father, Son and Holy Spirit have the same thoughts, goals and objectives. They have the same plan to achieve them, and they have all the power to do so. They are perfectly united operating in perfect harmony. All three are working in concert at the same time, accomplishing the same thing, sharing one existence. Only the dynamics (the ways of operation) of each is different.

53

THE WEIGHT OF GLORY

CHRIST IN US

As believers, we **carry** within us the manifested (very apparent) presence of the living God in the person of the Holy Ghost, who is the Spirit of Jesus Christ. Jesus Christ in us is the hope (realization) of glory. Jesus is the fullness of the Godhead bodily. That is, within Jesus is also God the Father and the Holy Spirit. Without the grace of God, it would be impossible for us to carry such a weight. **The weight of glory** is a fullness beyond measure. It is infinite and an endless blessedness.

THE WEIGHT OF IT

The Bible says God is from everlasting to everlasting; in other words, infinite. Carrying God is carrying infinity. How can we carry the weight of infinity? Although we are finite (limited) in our physical existence, we are actually infinite in our eternal lives. Although our human abilities are limited, the infinite Holy Spirit within us is not. He can do exceeding abundantly above all that we ask or think according to the power that He worketh in us. He is our unending unlimited source of power. He enables us to carry God's infinity on this earth in our mortal bodies. He gives us the strength so that it's not a burden. It's a joy.

OUR RESPONSIBILITY

We are ambassadors for Christ, making His appeal to the world to be reconciled to God. With this "charge" comes a responsibility. First, we must present our <u>body</u> as a living sacrifice, holy, acceptable unto God, which is our reasonable service. Holy Spirit helps us to do what is impossible without Him, but it is our responsibility to <u>be</u> <u>available</u> to Him. Without Christ, we can do nothing. We are to keep our <u>heart</u> with all diligence. And we are to endeavor to keep the unity of the <u>Spirit</u> and the bond of peace.

THE GLORY

The glory of God is the Shekinah, His radiant dwelling presence, in all of His power and majesty. Jesus Christ is the exact representation and express image of God. When we received Jesus as our Savior and Lord, we <u>received</u> the glory (the presence) of God. When we <u>give</u> God glory, we give honor and reverence to Him in worship and praise. The effects of His glory can be felt and seen physically and spiritually. It is impossible to stand in the manifested presence of the glory of God and not be affected.

HIS INFINITE WILL

Holy Spirit can enlighten our hearts so that we can know the infinite will of God concerning us. God's will is infinite because it spans and reaches in all directions and touches all things. Through Christ, we are empowered to do His will. We are infused with inner strength and confident peace. God, in his excellence, has provided everything we need. He's given us all spiritual blessings. He's given us all things that pertain to life and godliness. "Through Him we also have access by faith into this [remarkable state of] grace in which we [firmly and safely and securely] stand. **Let us rejoice in our hope** and the confident assurance **of [experiencing and enjoying] the glory of [our great] God** [the manifestation of His excellence and power]." (**Rom. 5:2 AMP**)

54

PRECIOUS HOLY SPIRIT

WHO IS HE?

Who is the Holy Spirit? **Gen. 1:2 KJV** says that He is the "Spirit of God". According to **John 14:17**, He is the "Spirit of Truth". **John 14:16 KJV** calls Him "Another Comforter". Through many scriptures in the Bible, we learn of His attributes. We learn that He is divine, wise, just and fearless, faithful, tender, quiet, gentile, persevering, liberating, saving, compassionate, longsuffering, burden-bearing and loving.

The same divine works that are ascribed to the Father and the Son are ascribed to the Holy Spirit. He was involved in creation and in the inspiration of the sacred scriptures, in the regeneration of fallen man, and in the resurrection of the body. He is co-eternal and co-existent with God the Father and God the Son.

WHY DO WE HAVE HIM?

Jesus said in John 14:18 that Holy Spirit came so we won't be comfortless. He came to strengthen us and to be our Advocate or Helper. He is our

Intercessor and Counselor. He is here to stand by us and be with us forever. He comes in answer to prayer. Christ gives Him to us. He is the promised gift of God.

WHY DO WE NEED HIM?

We need Holy Spirit because He is dynamic in executing the will of God. In other words, He is always active and working to carry out fully the plan of God, so that people are blessed, and God is glorified. Included in His power is the dispensing of Spiritual Gifts. Holy Spirit empowers us for service. The Holy Spirit bears witness with our spirit that we are the children of God. Holy Spirit is our teacher. He is our guide. By the in-filling of the Holy Spirit, we are enabled to speak in unknown languages. Holy Spirit controls the movements of believers that are totally yielded to Him. Holy Spirit chooses our field of operation, where He wants us to minister. The Holy Spirit giveth life. The Holy Spirit brings to our remembrance the words of Christ.

A NEW SPIRIT

If we are in Christ Jesus, Holy Spirit lives in us. Our bodies are the temple of the Holy Ghost, and we are not our own. When we experience cleansing and renewing of our spirits by the Holy Spirit, regeneration takes place. Through the Holy Spirit we are changed and born again to a new spirit. "Therefore if any man be in Christ, He is a new creature, old things are passed away; behold, all things are become new". (**2Cor. 5:17 KJV**) Jesus said to Nicodemus, "Except a man be born of water and of the Spirit, he cannot see the Kingdom of God. Marvel not that I said unto thee, ye must be born again." (**John 3:7 KJV**)

HIS BENEVOLENCE

God's love for us is expressed through the work of the Holy Spirit. The benevolence of the Holy Spirit goes beyond the Spiritual Gifts listed in

1Cor.12 and even beyond the Gifts of the Spirit in chapter 5 of Galatians. The benevolence of the Holy Spirit allows us the sweet communion with our God. It is by the Holy Spirit that we can come into the very presence of God and have a 1 on 1 personal relationship with the Father, the Son and the Holy Spirit.

God wills by His power. We receive through our trust and faith in Jesus. The Holy Spirit delivers what God wills for us to receive. All of the love, care, compassion, protection, wisdom, knowledge, understanding, healing and salvation is delivered to us by the Precious Holy Spirit.

55

AGREE AS TOUCHING

NOT A PHYSICAL TOUCH

"Again, I say unto you, that if two of you shall agree (**harmonize together**) on earth as touching anything that they shall ask, it shall be done for them of my Father which is in heaven." (**Matt. 18:19 KJV**} Notice that the scripture does not say if any of you touch and agree. This is not about physical touching.

Sometimes we can put a lot of emphasis on physical touching, for example, holding hands when we pray. Physical touching can be a way of connecting and sharing in the power that the prayer produces; however, it does not cause the power.

Although Mark 16:18 speaks about "laying hands" on the sick, 'and they shall recover', that is a manifestation of the signs that shall follow the believer. Also, note that touching or hands were "laid on" individuals for anointing, sending and specific functions and offices. These things are not what is being talked about in Matt. 18:19. It is not as much about physical touching as it is more about **spiritual touching**.

SAME BELIEF

The phrase "agree...as touching anything" is translated from the original **Greek** as meaning "with respect to", or "concerning a particular subject". So that to pray in agreement as touching anything on earth means to agree concerning a particular subject". In other words, the two persons need to be single-minded, on one accord, focused on and in expectation of a particular outcome of their prayer. There can be no room for doubt or unbelief. There can be no hedging or wondering of thoughts on that subject. They both (or all) have to trust and believe God for the answer to that prayer. Then let it be so. (Amen) Let God do it.

2Peter 1:1 KJV talks about "like precious faith". When we are praying in agreement, we must have that same kind of precious faith. That is having the same confidence in God, believing Him for the prayer request whole-heartedly. There can be no "what ifs", no "maybe". A half-hearted agreement is no agreement at all. In unity (agreement) God commands a blessing. Our spirits must be steadfast, and we must have enough love and willingness to trust God for anything.

BOLD FAITH

We don't have to be afraid or timid about coming into an agreement with someone in prayer, as long as the prayer lines up with the word of God.

1John 5:14 KJV says, "And this is the confidence that we have in Him, that, if we ask any thing according to His will, He heareth us: and if we know that He hear us, whatsoever we ask, we know that we have the petitions that we desired of Him.".

According to 2Cor. 4:13-15, if we believe something, we will speak it. We must have the same spirit of faith, being assured and convinced that God's divine favor and spiritual blessing will be extended to us when we pray.

Again in **Rom.10:9-10 KJV,** it tells us that believing and speaking go together. "That if thou shalt confess with thy mouth the Lord Jesus, and shalt believe in thine heart that God has raised Him from the dead, thou shalt be saved."

REMEMBER

Remember that Jesus put doubters out of the room. It is important for us not to seek a doubter to pray the prayer of agreement with. Anyone who wants us to diminish our expectations from God will hinder a prayer of agreement. Do not pray the prayer of agreement with them.

56

THE BREATH OF GOD

LIFE GIVER

John 6:63 KJV says "It is the Spirit that quickeneth; the flesh profiteth nothing: the words that I speak unto you, they are Spirit, and they are life." This verse says that God's words are Spirit; which is derived from the Hebrew word "pneuma" meaning "breath" or the "Holy Spirit" or "life". The word "life" in the Hebrew is zoe meaning "life" or "lifetime". So here, God is saying that His words are His living breath, animated. The beginning of this verse says "it is the Spirit that quickeneth, (makes alive; gives life).

THE BREATH OF LIFE

Gen. 2:7 KJV says, "And the Lord God formed man of the dust of the ground and <u>breathed</u> into His nostrils <u>the breath of life</u>, and man became a living soul".

We want to see the partnership of His words with His breath. The breath of God executes the Word of God. When God speaks, His words give life to whoever or whatever He is directing them to.

Another incident of God breathing out the Holy Spirit or the life-giving Spirit is found in **John 20:22 KJV**, which says, "And when He had said this, He breathed on them, and saith unto them, Receive ye the Holy Ghost." Jesus said this to the disciples to empower them as He sent them out to do His work. The Bible attests to the partnership between God's words and His breath. 2Tim. 3:16 says, all scripture is God-breathed, meaning comes out from God.

When God speaks or breathes out words, things happen. By the Word of the Lord were the heavens made; and all the hosts of them by the <u>breath</u> of His mouth. (**Ps.33:6**)

LIGHT OVER DARKNESS

God can breathe (through His Words) on any dead area or situation in our lives and bring light to them. No matter if the situations are pertaining to unsaved souls, disastrous situations, bereavement over loved ones, depression, bondage, infirmities, financial lack, legal problems or any darkness in our spirits. God can bring life to it. **John 1:4-5 (AMP)** says, "<u>In Him (the Word) was life, and the life was the light of men.</u> And the light shineth in darkness; and the darkness has never overpowered it". The life in God's words overcomes any darkness in our lives.

BREATHING IN LIFE

We need to purpose in our hearts to "breathe in" or receive the life that God's Word gives. When we fully receive God's Word into our spirit, it will become flesh, a part of our spirit, body and soul, so that we are affected by it.

This effect is evidenced in the way we live our lives. If the Word has become flesh in us, it has control over what we do and how we do it. In other words, it begins to redefine who we are. The Word of God becomes alive in us, and we begin to live by our faith and trust in God, not in ourselves.

We realize that we are not fit or sufficient of ourselves, but our sufficiency comes from God. We cannot have spiritual life just by knowing the letter of the law which gives no life, (that is, the actual words on the page). When we breathe in or receive the breath of God, we receive the spiritual life that is in His Word, for the "letter killeth, but the Spirit giveth life."(**2Cor. 3:5-6 KJV**) Let the breath of God continue to give us life.

57

INVESTING IN GOD

A COMMITMENT TO INVEST

Investment is a commitment. To invest is to use, give, or devote...as for a purpose to achieve something. If you are willing to invest money, time or effort into a person or thing and to carry it through, this shows that you believe that the promised outcome will come to pass. Our commitment to invest should have begun when we were saved. (Rom. 10:9-10) There is a promise or something to be gained by investing our trust in God. **Pro.3:5-6** says, "Trust in the Lord with all of your heart and lean not unto your own understanding. In all your ways acknowledge Him, and He shall direct your path". We want God to direct our paths, but if we have not invested trust in Him, we cannot receive direction from Him.

PROOF OF VALUE OF THE INVESTMENT

We can invest our trust in God's Word because its value is solid and permanent. All of the promises (the Word) of God in Christ are yea and Amen. Actually, the more that we invest in it, the more the value increases. **Is. 45:23 KJV** says, "1 have <u>sworn</u> by myself" (being the highest authority of this universe). The Word is gone out of my mouth in righteousness and shall not return". **2Tim.3:16-17 KJV** guarantees the authenticity of His Word, saying that, "All scripture is given by inspiration of God, and is profitable for doctrine, for reproof, for correction, for instruction in righteousness...".

The proof of the value of the Word of God that we invest our trust in is in Heb. 6:13-18, where He confirms the immutability (unchangeable nature) of His counsel (His Word) by swearing an oath that He adds on to the promise already made. This gives even stronger reassurance that His Word is true. His Word is perfect, right, righteous altogether, and more desirable than gold. Ultimately, God Himself is the guarantor of the value and validity of His Word.

RETURN ON THE INVESTMENT

Investing our trust in the Lord is profitable because He alone meets all our needs. John 10:10 says Jesus has come that we might have life and that more abundantly. We know that He is Jehovah Jireh, Our Provider. If we invest or commit all of our trust in Him, we have the benefits of all the promises of God in Christ. Our confidence must be in Him at all times. We must be "all in" with our trust in God. His Word is not a gamble. It is a sure thing. To reap the full value of our investment, we must be totally sold out to God, leaving no room for doubt. He must have our fully committed trust, no matter what we see or feel. There should be no "Plan B", no "what ifs". We must trust Him for all things—in every situation, believing that all things are working together for our good. There can be no wavering. The Bible says in James 1:6-7, that any man who wavers in faith should not expect to receive anything from the Lord. We must make a 100% investment; no holding back of anything. Then we will receive a return from the Lord of some thirty, some sixty, and some hundred times the amount that we invested.

DAILY INVESTMENT

Investing trust in God is something we should do daily to receive our daily benefits. Daily benefits gives us the power to conquer whatever the enemy throws at us each day. Matt.6:34 says that each day has enough trouble of its own for us to deal with.

Investing trust in God is not a one-time thing. It is a treasure we continue to add to. **Matt. 6:19-20 KJV** says, "But lay up for yourselves treasures in heaven...not upon earth." We need to set our minds on investing in the Most High God. Our trust in Him <u>will never fail to pay off</u>.

58

A SPIRITUAL MARRIAGE COVENANT

THE UNION

In the natural, marriage is an intimate and usually permanent union or relation between two persons, as designated by God ; to wed. Covenant is a formal and serious <u>agreement </u>or promise between two persons. So, a marriage covenant is a serious <u>promise</u> of devotion with an intent to wed. The marriage **union** is consummated or completed on the day of the wedding. Spiritually speaking, **Rev. 19:7 AMP** says, "Let us rejoice and shout for joy. Let us celebrate and ascribe to Him glory and honor, for the marriage of the Lamb has come, and His bride has prepared herself." "As the bridegroom rejoices over the bride, so shall your God rejoice over you." **(Is.62:5 KJV)**

THE BRIDE

The church is the <u>bride</u> of Christ. The whole church is one body in Christ. Christ is the head of the church. The whole body of believers will be presented to Christ as a virgin.

WEDDING DAY

A wedding day is coming. One of the angels in Rev. 21:9 told John to "come" so he could show him the Lamb's wife, God's people, (of the new Jerusalem) adorned for her husband.

Historically, during consummation of the marriage with a virgin bride, blood is spilled, as full intimacy and <u>covenant</u> of the relationship is confirmed.

JESUS THE MEDIATOR

A mediator is like a negotiator or go-between. Jesus had to shed His blood so as to mediate the new covenant (or <u>agreement</u>) so that its promises would be received by the saints (His bride).

In the past, it was customary when ratifying a <u>covenant or pledge</u>, for an animal to be cut in to two halves, and the two making the covenant, to pass between the two parts. However, Jesus' blood ratified (confirmed) the covenant made between God and His people. "And for this cause He is the mediator of the new testament, that by means of death, for the redemption of the transgressions that were under the first testament, they which are called might receive the promise of eternal <u>inheritance.</u>" (**Heb.9:15 KJV**)

SANCTIFIED

The church is subject to its head, which is Christ. Jesus loved us so much that He gave Himself up for us. In doing that He was able to sanctify us and clean us up by the washing of water with the Word. At the appointed time, Jesus will present the church to Himself in glorious splendor, not having spot or wrinkle, or any such thing, but holy and without blemish.

DOXOLOGY

To those who were chosen to be sanctified and consecrated by the Holy Spirit unto obedience and to be sprinkled with the blood of Jesus Christ, who are kept by the power of God through faith, until you fully <u>inherit</u> that final salvation that is ready to be revealed for you in the last time, grace and peace be multiplied.

"Now unto Him that is able to keep you from falling, and to present you faultless before the presence of His glory with exceeding joy, To the only wise God our Savior, be glory and majesty, dominion and power, both now and ever". Amen (**Jude 24-25 KJV**)

59

SUFFICIENCY IN GOD

SOURCE AND SUPPLY

"But my God shall supply all your need according to His riches in glory by Christ Jesus." (**Phil. 4:19 KJV**) If we are obedient and compassionate enough to meet the needs of others, we don't have to worry about going lacking ourselves. In Phil. 4:18, Paul is acknowledging the gifts and financial support he received from the Philippian church and assuring them that because they have been so generous to him and have given sacrificially, that they have pleased God, and God will, for their sacrifices, meet their need. God is **the source and the supply** of our need. "Every good gift and every perfect gift is from above, and cometh down from the Father of lights, with whom is no variableness, neither shadow of turning." (**James 1:17 KJV**) He is consistent.

ADDING THINGS

Matt. 6:33 KJV says, "But seek ye first the Kingdom of God, and His righteousness, and **all these things** (your need) **shall be added** unto you". From Matt.6:32, we see that God already knows that we need food, and clothes and shelter, so we don't have to devote ourselves to acquiring them. He shall supply those things if we focus ourselves on seeking and doing those things which He describes as righteous in His Word. Love God and love thy neighbor as thyself. Help the poor, the widows, visit the fatherless, keep ourselves holy. This is pure religion.

NO SUFFICIENCY IN OURSELVES

Of ourselves, we have no sufficiency, but our sufficiency is of God. Without Him, we can do nothing. God is able to make every favor and earthly (grace) blessing come to us in abundance so we can be sufficient for every good work and charitable donation. With this knowledge we have the confidence that no matter what state of poverty or prosperity we are in, to be content, for **His grace is sufficient** for us.

Phil. 4:13 AMP says, "I have strength for all things in Christ Who empowers me [I am ready for anything and equal to anything through Him Who infuses inner strength into me; I am self-sufficient in Christ's sufficiency]". What this is saying is that I am always over-abundantly supplied **by Him**.

OUR SHEPHERD

The Lord is our shepherd who feeds, guides and protects us. We shall lack for nothing. The Shepherd, **Jehovah Rohi**, sees our needs and has made plans already to fulfill them. Isaiah 41:10 says that He will help us and uphold us with right hand of His righteousness. God is always with us. We are never alone in our need, for He promised never to leave nor forsake us. Also, He has given angels charge over us to keep us in all our ways.

MORE THAN ENOUGH

If we put our faith in the Lord and believe that He will fully equip us for every situation, we will surely have the victory continually, for He always causes us to triumph in Christ. He will take what we have and make it more than sufficient. The power released from the Lord's crucifixion and resurrection produces more than enough grace for our every need.

God is **El Shaddai**, the Almighty God. He is self-existent, self-sufficient and all-sovereign. He has everything we need to meet any situation. "Now let Him that is able to do exceeding abundantly above all that we ask or think, according to the power that (He) worketh in us" (**Eph.3:20 KJV**), let Him be the almighty God that He is. Let us trust Him, the everlasting God, to be the "I AM", (whatever) we need.

60

COME

TO THE THRONE

Our God is a God of love. "God is love". (**1John 4:8 KJV**) Because He loves us, God gave us free will to Love Him back. He does not make us, but time after time He asks us to **come** to Him so that He can share His love with us. He has promises to keep towards us and does not desire that any of us should perish. God shares His love by giving to us. In Heb. 4:16, it says that we are invited (exhorted) to **come** boldly to the throne of grace to obtain mercy and to find grace to help in time of need.

FOLLOW HIM

In Mark 1:17, Jesus exhorts us to **come** and follow after Him and He will make us fishers of men, witnessing and teaching His truths. In Matt. 14:29, again Jesus encourages us to step out on the water and **come** to Him, so we can receive the rewards of having strong faith. Although the ground may look like water, when we step out, it will become as solid as our faith and trust in Him. And in Matt. 11:28, Jesus says to **come** unto Him, and He will give us rest. My sheep hear my voice, and they follow Me.

COME CLOSE

God is always working out His good plans for us. He is always directing us where we can get our needs met. He directs us to **come** to Him for a place of safety. We are able to **come** for Godly fellowship. We are able to **come** for personal salvation. If we accept His free gift of eternal life, we can **come** to the waters (the living waters) and drink freely. If we submit and consent to His divine will, we can **come**, and He will revive our souls.

THE CALL

The invitation is extended to everyone. The wedding banquet is prepared. All things are ready. When we hear God calling us to **come,** let us not harden our hearts and treat His invitation with contempt by ignoring it. We must heed the call of wisdom and answer the call. (**Pro.1:24 KJV**)

A 3-FOLD CALL

In Rev. 22:17AMP, there is a 3-fold call to us to **come**. First, from the Holy Spirit. Second, from the "bride". That is, the true Christians (the church). Thirdly, it says, let anyone that is listening say **come**. Whosoever will, let Him **come**. Let everyone **come** who is thirsty [who is painfully conscious of his need of those things by which the soul is refreshed, supported and strengthened]; and whoever [earnestly] desires to do it, let Him **come**, take, use, and drink the water of Life without cost.

IN THE HOUSE

"I was glad when they said unto me, let us go (**come**) into the house of the Lord." (**Ps. 122:1 AMP**) All whom my Father gives (entrusts) to Me will **come** to Me; and the one who **comes** to Me I will most certainly not cast out [I will never, no never, reject one of them who **comes** to Me]

A PERPARED PLACE

Jesus has prepared a place for us. He anticipates our **coming** there to be with Him. "The Lord thy God in the midst of thee is mighty; He will save, He will rejoice over thee with joy; He will rest in His love, He will joy over thee with singing". (**Zeph. 3:17 KJV**) Our place in Him is reserved. No man shall pluck us out of His hand. We have only to **come**

61

SPIRITUAL KINSHIP

A HOUSEHOLD

In Gal. 6:10 (AMP), it tells us that we should be especially good to those who are in the family [household] of believers [faith]. A household in this sense means those that adhere to (are loyal to) a leader's set of principles or are believers in those principles. Being especially good or kind to them means forbearing one another in love and "endeavoring to keep the unity of the Spirit and the bond of peace". (**Eph. 4:3 KJV**)

RELATIVES

In the title, "Spiritual Kinship", we are talking about spiritual relatives. "But to as many as did receive and welcome Him, He gave the authority (power, privilege, right) to become the children of God, that is, to those who believe in (adhere to, trust in, and rely on) His name---Who <u>owe their birth</u> neither to bloods nor to the will of the flesh [that of physical impulse] nor to the will of man [that of a natural father], but <u>to God.</u> [They are born of God!]" (**John 1:12-13 AMP**)

BLOOD LINE

So basically, we are saying that the relative in the household is a relative by virtue of His birth into the family. There is therefore, a genetic line that leads back to the spiritual Father, which is God. Jesus' DNA (His blood) must be running (spiritually) through their veins.

SAME FATHER

We are to take special care of our spiritual relatives, our kin. We are fitly joined together in just the right way for that purpose. "The Spirit itself beareth witness with our spirits that we are the children of God.: And if children, then heirs; heirs of God, and joint-heirs with Christ..." (**Rom. 8:16-17 KJV**)

COMMON EXPERIENCES

Oftentimes, the bond that holds family members together is the common experiences that they have gone through, some planned and some unplanned. As a result of this, mutual love, understanding and support for one another takes place. In 2Pet.1:1, 3-4 AMP, some planned divine common experiences are listed that believers can build a bond upon. In this verse it says that we (believers) have received like (the same) precious faith together with ourselves in and through the righteousness of our God and Savior Jesus Christ. We have also received all things that pertain to life and godliness. Lastly, it says that we have all received His precious and exceedingly great promises, that we may be partakers of the divine nature (not our carnal nature), having escaped the corruption that is in the world because of lust and greed.

SPIRITUAL FAMILY

Who is our spiritual family? Can you identify your spiritual kin? Can your spirit bear witness with their spirit? Is it the people we spend a lot of time with? Is it the ones we admire and want to be like? Is it the ones we've known the longest? Is it our natural sisters, brothers, mothers, fathers?

In **Mark 3:33-35,** Jesus answers the question. He says in verse 35, "For whoever does the things my God wills is my brother and sister and mother." So, we must stop claiming individuals as our spiritual mother, father, sister or brother if their lifestyle does not line up with the will of God. We are to try (prove) the spirit to see whether they are of God.

Whoever is of God listens to God. [Those who belong to God hear the words of God.] This is the reason that you do not listen [to those words, to Me]: because you do not belong to God and are not of God or in harmony with Him."

62

IT IS WELL

A DECLARATION OF FAITH

In 2Kings 4:12-26, there was a Shunammite woman who had set up a room to accommodate the many visits of Elisha, the man of God, to her house. Her grown son got sick and died. This was the son that Elisha had promised her in appreciation for her being so hospitable to him. Upon hearing his promise, she asked him not to deceive her in delivering his promise. So, a year after the promise, she gave birth to a son.

After her son died, she went to where Elisha was. When Elisha saw her coming, he sent his servant to ask her was it well with her, with her husband, and with her child. She answered, "It is well".

How could she say that when her son had just died? This was a declaration of faith in the man of God, who had promised her a son. She would not believe that he would deceive her by letting her raise him up only just to die. So, she made the journey to see Elisha. When she got there, she grabbed ahold to his feet and reminded him of his promise to her. Her actions were based on her absolute faith that the man of God was able to revive her dead son. Therefore, she had answered, "It is well", on her way there.

LESSONS

There are many lessons to be learned here. One is to "Have faith in God". (**Mark 11:22 KJV**) Another is to, "Walk by faith, not by sight". (**2Cor.5:7**) According to **Ps.37:5**, we are to "commit our way unto the Lord". Here, commit means to trust Him enough to obligate or pledge oneself and one's course of life, unto the Lord.

How much are we ready to pledge the way we live our lives unto the Lord? We must know in our hearts that God has all power, and He is fully in charge. Then we too can have the assurance and confidence to say in any situation that, "It is well".

SELF-ENCOURAGEMENT

Sometimes we have to encourage ourselves in the Lord. That means to remind ourselves what the Lord says in His Word. Like the Shunammite woman did, grab ahold to His feet and don't let go. Cast down any negative thoughts that are contrary to His Word. Think positive thoughts. Stand on His promises. Rebuke the devil's fear tactics, and walk in power, love and a strong mind. Avoid negative speaking people. Totally confuse the enemy by giving God praise and worship because "It is well with your soul", as the song says. Continue in the Lord, in prayer and in the meditation and study of His Word.

STILL WELL

Everyone deals with challenges in life. It may seem that the devil is always throwing problems at us. If we're ok in one area, we have trouble in another. In spite of the imperfections of life, "It is still well" because God is still God. We must never forget the grace in which we stand by faith in Jesus Christ. The grace is the state of God's favor. God favors us.

BECAUSE OF HIS GRACE

Because He favors us, He will still provide for us. He is still our Healer. He is still our protector. He is the Lifter of our heads and the Lover of our souls. We are the apple of His eye. His mind is full of thoughts about us. His plans for us are good and not evil for a good outcome for us. By the grace of God, "It is Well"!

63

SOVEREIGN

SOVEREIGN OVER THE WORLD

God is sovereign over the world. What does sovereign mean? It means He has total authority and unlimited power to govern Himself. Nobody governs God or controls God or hinders God from what He wants to do. **Ps 115:3AMP** says, "But our God is in heaven. He does whatever He pleases." The Lord reignest over all. In His hand is power and might. "For God hath power to help, and to cast down". (**2Chron. 25:8 KJV**) "Power belongeth unto God". (**Ps.62:11**)

Who are we to question Him or doubt Him? He made us. We didn't make ourselves. We cannot question our creator as to why He made us the way He did. He doesn't have to answer to us or anyone else. We cannot council (or advise) Him on what we don't understand. His thoughts and ways are way above our human abilities to comprehend.

SOVEREIGN OVER TIME

God is sovereign over time. "The Lord appointed the moon for the seasons. The sun knows [the exact time of] its setting". (**Ps.104:19 AMP**) **Dan. 2:21** says, "He changes the times and the seasons." Our times are in His hand. God has given a season or time for everything. He has given a time to be born. Our birth was planned to happen just at the time it did. He gave a time or season to plant and a time to pluck up that which is planted. This illustrates a spiritual law as well as a natural one. We learn that if we plant seeds of the Word in the good ground of our hearts, then there will come a harvest of faith.

God has also given a time to kill (for food or protection) and a time to heal (emotional wounds, broken hearts, physical bodies and estranged relationships). He gave a time to break down, and a time to build up. Some things need to be destroyed so that the new (and better) can be built up.

God's time is relevant, depending on His use of it for His own purpose. Remember, "one day is with the Lord as a thousand years, and a thousand years as one day". (**2Pet.3:8 KJV**) So we must be mindful of this while we are waiting on God. Let us wait with patience trusting that He knows exactly when to manifest those things we were praying for.

SOVERIGN OVER SPACE

God is sovereign over space and everything in it. "For by Him were all things created that are in heaven, and that are in earth, visible and invisible, whether they be thrones, or dominions, or principalities, or powers (angelic rankings): all things were created by Him". (**Col. 1:16 KJV**)

God has all the forces of nature in His control, including the sun, moon, stars and planets. God told the sea to come this far and no further. Only God commands the wind and the rain. He can unleash or restrain them at will. Instead of asking God questions about what He is doing, we need to recognize and submit to God's power and sovereignty.

SOVEREIGN OVER THE CIRCUMSTANCES OF OUR LIVES

The next time we are tempted to complain to God about our circumstances, remember this. From His high position (above the circle of the earth), He orchestrates the beautiful and perfect order of things.

Although we have freedom of choice, God will do all He can to help us make the right choices that will coincide with His will for our lives. **2Pet.2:9 KJV** says, "The Lord knoweth how to deliver the godly out of temptations, and to reserve the unjust unto the day of judgement to be punished."

64

BONDAGE

WHAT IS BONDAGE?

Bondage is the state of being a slave; yoked up; servitude. Are we a servant of Satan, a slave to sin? **Rom. 8:15 KJV** says, "For ye have not received the **spirit of bondage** again to fear; but ye have received the Spirit of adoption whereby we cry, Abba, Father." We have been adopted by God and are now free of Satan's hold on us.

So, what do we do? Go back and yoke ourselves up again and make Satan our master? God forbid. "But now, after that ye have known God, or rather are known of God, how turn ye again to the weak and beggarly elements of this world (all religions before Christ came) whereunto ye desire again to be in bondage?" (**Gal.4:9 KJV**) Why would we want that again?

TEMPTATIONS

God does not lead anyone into temptation. Temptation to do wrong is not from God. It was not God who told us to make that purchase that we couldn't afford, or to eat that dessert that we didn't need, or to play that lottery number that He didn't give.

"But every man is tempted, when he is drawn away of his own lust, and enticed". (**James 1:14 KJV**) This is us falling victim to our own lusts and enticing our own selves to give in to the temptation.

NO LONGER SLAVES

It is a helpless feeling of being controlled by something you have no power over, However, because of Christ's victory over Satan, Jesus has gotten us the victory. We are no longer slaves to sin. Iniquity no longer has dominion over us.

Now we can choose to live out our freedom of choice. The Lord has given us an opportunity each day to choose death or life. Choosing bondage is self-destructive because lust leads to sin, and the end result of sin is death (spiritual or natural).

THE DEVIL'S AIM

The devil's objectives have not changed. He still seeks to steal, kill, and destroy God's people. We must not be fooled at how he dresses up the temptation, the negative effect on us will be the same. Once we yield to any temptation, it becomes easier and easier to do so. Herein lies the bondage. It's not that the devil has power over us, but we have given over to him our power that Jesus died for. "For all that is in the world, the lust of the flesh, the lust of the eyes, and the pride of life, is not of the Father, but is of the world." (**1John 2:16 KJV**)

JESUS' AIM

Jesus' objective has not changed. He has come that we **might** have life, and that we **might** have it more abundantly. Notice it says "might". Abundant life is made available to us by the work of Jesus Christ, but we still can choose death instead. Remember the end result of sin is death. The spirit of bondage is the Strongman in this warfare against us. He sends out his demons to attack us. Their assignments are to tie us up in fetters and chains so that we cannot obey God. These **evil spirits** appeal to the flesh and to the soul (mind, will, and emotions). Some are various kinds of addictions: some sexual, some to food, cigarettes (or smoking anything), drug abuse, even to people. Others can be laziness, lying, thievery, low self-esteem, depression, anger, fear, pride idolatry, rejection, religious spirits, violence, hatred, profanity, gambling, debt and perversion of God's Word. Anything that influences you to operate outside of God's will for you is bondage. "Stand therefore in the liberty wherewith Christ hath made us free, and be not entangled again with the yoke of bondage" (**Gal. 5:1 KJV**)

65

THE WORD "FOR"

WHAT DOES IT MEAN?

The word "**For**" is used many times in the Bible and is often used to begin certain declarations. A declaration is the act of making an official statement about something; an announcement; an affirmation. When these affirmations are made, the word "**For**" is used to underscore or strongly emphasize the truth about something being declared. The definitions of the word "For", in these instances, mean: because, seeing that, on account of, for the reason that, by virtue of the fact that, in as much as, since, indeed, therefore, the truth is, assuredly.

PSALMS 100:5

Even though "For" is a small word, we should not neglect to recognize that its use holds a lot of meaning and revelation. For example, in the phrase, "**For the Lord is good.…**" (**Ps. 100:5 KJV**), we could just say 'yes, we know God is good', and leave it at that. But if we substitute some of the meanings of "**For**", it will reveal or open up a lot more to our understanding. Thus, it might read like this with additional revelations as follows:

"Since" **the Lord is good**" ..., certain things are expected.

"The fact is that" the Lord is good..., so we know something about His character.

"Seeing that" the Lord is good..., evil things don't apply to Him.

"Indeed" the Lord is good" ..., that's a true fact.

JOHN 3:16

Let's look at another example. "**For God so loved the world...**" (**John 3:16 KJV**) Substituting additional meanings of "For", we get more.

"Since" **God so loved the world**...anticipation of a result.

"Because" God so loved the world...This gives us the reason for His sacrifice.

"Assuredly" God so loved the world..., Without a doubt, we can be sure that; it is absolutely true.

ISAIAH 9:6

"**For unto us a child is born...**" (**Is. 9:6 KJV**) Another way it might read is,

"For the reason that" **unto us a child is born** .... This would have us to focus on the child being "for" us. We receive Him as a gift from God.

"Because" ...unto us a child is born, certain benefits to us will be received.

"The truth is that" unto us a child is born..., This affirms the event as a fact, a reality that may stir up a since of awe and gratitude.

ROMANS 6:23

"**For the wages of sin is death**…," (**Rom. 6:23 KJV**) Substitute for the word "For".

"On account of the fact that" **the wages of sin is death**…. Because this is the truth, take heart; heed the warning.

"Assuredly" …the wages of sin is death. Be it known to everyone that hears this. There's no escaping. The wages or consequences of sin will be paid by you or by someone you impact.

1JOHN 4:4

"**For greater is He that is in you…**" (1John4:4 KJV)

"Because" **Greater is He that is in you** means that's why we will always have the victory.

"Since" Greater is He that is in you… Then you don't have to worry about the devil's tactics against you.

"Assuredly" Greater is He that is in you… means you've got to know it for a fact, without a doubt. So, there is no need for fear.

BY EVERY WORD

There is so much in every word of scripture. Each word is packed with much more meaning than is first seen on the surface. It is necessary to dive deep sometimes so as to catch a deeper meaning. God's words are important. We should not take any of them lightly. "…Hear the Words of the Lord your God". (**Josh. 3:9 KJV**) If we pay attention, we will see that God is purposeful and deliberate in all that He does and in all that He says.

66

WITH THANKSGIVING

THANKSGIVING IS A PRAYER

"Be careful for nothing; but in everything <u>by prayer</u> and supplication <u>with thanksgiving</u> let your requests be made known unto God. And the peace of God, which passeth all understanding, shall keep your hearts and minds through Christ Jesus." (**Phil.4:6 KJV**)

"Thanksgiving" is a prayer. When we give thanks to God, we are communicating to Him our gratitude for the gifts…whether small or large. It is a one-on-one, face-to-face act of humility for His continued faithfulness towards us. It shows that we appreciate what He has done, and we don't take Him for granted. It is an act of honor and affection for Him as our benefactor.

THANKSGIVING IS A WORSHIP

It is a worship because it is a demonstration of our belief in who He is. We must believe that He is God. When we give thanks unto God, we are acknowledging His sovereignty and intentional kindness towards us. It is a sacrifice of praise with the fruit of our lips giving thanks to His name. We are giving Him full credit for being the One and Only God responsible for every grace afforded us and for every blessing showered upon us. We know that nothing happens by chance, but all things and events are subject to His authority to permit or disallow them. Therefore, when He orchestrates the events of our lives in a way that gives us comfort and joy, we are grateful, because these things did not have to come out in our favor.

GIVING THANKS GIVES US PEACE

When we diligently offer our thanks to God, we will have a peace that passes all understanding. This is a peace that does not necessarily reflect our present circumstances, but it is an inner peace. It is a satisfaction of having given God what He is due and feeling good about it. The more thanks we give, the more peace we will have.

KEEPS HEARTS AND MINDS

When our hearts and minds are filled with thanksgiving, there is no room left for sorrow, depression, sadness or self-pity. Instead, joy fills our hearts and minds. Praise fills our mouths. Our feet want to dance. Our spirits want to soar. Our hands are lifted up to God. The enemy is blocked from entering.

THROUGH CHRIST JESUS

It is in or through Christ Jesus that this promise is fulfilled. With Christ nothing shall be impossible. "…With God all things are possible." (**Matt.19:26 KJV**) In Him our requests are granted, and His peace is imparted. This is the only way or avenue to receiving the promises of God.

Jesus Christ says, "I am the way..." (**John 14:6 KJV**) We are to live our lives daily in Christ Jesus being thankful for His perpetual mercies and grace. **Isaiah 30:21AMP** says, "...this is the way, walk ye in it..."

When we find ourselves not in a place of peace, let us turn back to the "way" that Jesus has provided for us. Let us cast off any anxiety or worry. Let us refuse to entertain any thoughts of fear or defeat.

67

CORRUPT COMMUNICATION

HURTING YOURSELF

Eph.4:29 KJV – "Let no corrupt communication proceed out of your mouth, but that which is good to the use of edifying, that it may minister grace unto the hearers." Corrupt communication means more than using profanity. It means saying anything hurtful, evil, vicious, malicious, bad, offensive, rotten things, that will tear down, or that will destroy. These things should not proceed out of our mouths.

What comes out of our mouth reflects what lies deep in our hearts. **Matt. 12:34 KJV** tells us this. "For out of the abundance of the heart, the mouth speaketh." When evil thoughts, murders (words of hate), adulteries, fornications, thefts, false witness, blasphemies proceed out of the heart, these are the things which defile a person. Defile means to contaminate, dishonor, make impure. Therefore, the Lord teaches us in **Ps.34:13 KJV** to "keep our tongues from evil, and our lips from speaking guile" (treachery, deceit and lies). He knows that we defile our own selves when we speak corrupt words or thoughts. When we are trying to hurt someone with words, we are defiling our own bodies and spirits. This is why many are sick physically and spiritually. The tongue contaminates and poisons the whole body. "A man's moral self shall be filled with the fruit of his mouth, and with the consequences of his words he must be satisfied [whether good or evil]. Death and life are in the power of the tongue, and they who indulge in it shall eat the fruit of it [for death or life]." (**Pro.18:20-21 AMP**)

HELPING OTHERS

The Word tells us that we are to use our communication only for the purpose of speaking or accomplishing "good", that which is "helpful for building others up according to their needs, that it may benefit those who listen." (**Eph.4:29 Life App**) The way to be sure you are following this directive is found by speaking only in agreement with God's Word, deliberately choosing words that will empower the hearers for advancement and victory in their lives, words that will be an encouragement to them. God says, choose life, so that you and your descendants may live. Speak life to everyone that you come into contact with based on the Word of God. The Bible says, you have what you say.

YOU CHOOSE

Remember, it only takes a spark to set off a forest fire. By our speech, we can ruin the world, turn harmony to chaos, throw mud on a reputation, send the whole world up in smoke The only way to control our tongue is to keep silent, unless we can say something edifying. The tongue's deceitfulness is ignited by Hell. With the tongue, we bless the Lord and Father, and with it we curse men who were made in God's likeness.

Righteousness is doing God's will in thought and deed. It is God's will that we be peace-makers sowing peace with our words. We want our communication to be pure, true and conformed to God's will and purpose. We have to intentionally choose to bless and not curse people with our tongues. That means, we need to think and pray before we speak. If we acknowledge (seek) God concerning what we shall say, He will direct us in what to say and how to say it.

Speak the Word. It is spirit and it is life. It will not kill, but it will make alive. It will not tear down, but it will build up. It will speak truth, and it will not lie. This applies to you, the speaker, as well as to who you are speaking to or about. "By your words, you will be justified (found innocent), and by your words, you shall be condemned sentenced)". (**Matt. 12:37 AMP**) So, watch what you say.

68

LIFE

ORIGIN OF LIFE

Life started from **God's will**. He willed our lives into existence before the foundation of the world. Life came out of God, the Self-Existing One, the One who says, "I AM that I AM". (**Ex.3:14 KJV**), the One who said, "LET THERE BE…", and there was! (**Gen.1:3 KJV**) He is, and always was, and forever will be. He is the Almighty, the Ruler of all.

PHYSICAL LIFE

God is the owner and creator of life. He created physical life. People, animals and plants have physical life. Physical life is characterized by growing and producing after its own kind.

SPIRITUAL LIFE

Spiritual life is the part of man's existence that belongs to his **soul.** Only people have a soul. "And the Lord formed man out of the dust of the ground and breathed into his nostrils the breath (or spirit) of life; and man became a living **soul**". (**Gen.2:7 KJV**) All created beings have life from God, but only mankind has the spiritual, Godkind of life (zoe).

The spirit, soul and body make up the human life. God has made us with three aspects, as He, Himself is three (or triune). He is God the Father, God the Son and God the Holy Spirit. The **soul** of man is his mind, will and emotions. Man's mind, will, and emotions need to be surrendered to God for God to control. It is a voluntary thing to do from the heart. It is done through prayer, worship, study of His Word, meditation on His Word, and obedience to His Word. Man's spirit and soul came from God and will be returned to God after this physical life is done. Blessed be the name of Our God!

LIFE SPAN

Since God owns life (He has the patent on it), He has the right to designate its purpose, for His own glory. He also has the right to designate when it shall come to an end. Life, itself, belongs to God. Only He has the right to give it or to take it away. We don't have any claim on our life, as it was only lent to us out of the graciousness of God, for a time. God is due all the glory for any victory or anything positive we might have accomplished during our life span. We shall not covet life, ours nor anyone else's. We do need to be good stewards of it because our life span, the time between birth and death, is God's gift to us, and it is precious.

LIFE STYLE

When we believe that Jesus died for our sins on the cross and rose again, we receive the right to spiritual eternal life with Him, His Father and the Holy Spirit in heaven. However, eternal life begins while we are still here on earth. Our new life in Christ (our salvation) and the changes it brings should be evident. God has given us the free will to believe or not, to follow Him or not, to obey His Word or not. The wrong choice brings consequences. Thereby, we are allowed to determine our eternal fate.

Even though God has great plans for our life, each day we must make life decisions as to what way or manner (our lifestyle) we choose to live. Each day we get to make a choice that will either lead to <u>life or to death.</u> Let us choose JESUS. He is the way, the truth and the life. He is our life. There are two ways that we can choose to live the life that God has given us. We can choose to live life <u>controlled by our flesh or by the Spirit of God.</u> Living life in the flesh means being controlled by me, myself and I. But **Gal. 5:16 AMP** tells us, "…walk (live) in the Spirit, and ye shall not fulfill the lusts (cravings of human nature without God) of the flesh." So, let us choose to be controlled by the Spirit of God and live our lives daily in this liberty to choose to please Him.

69

IT'S TIME

GOD CREATED TIME FOR US

God did not create time for Himself. God created time for us. God operates outside of time, outside of its limitations. God is not directed or controlled by time. Time is controlled by God. God created time as boundaries for us to operate in and live by and as a tool of measurement for us to use. We are subject to time's limitations unless God intervenes to redeem it, slow it down, speed it up or halt it altogether.

REDEEMING TIME

God can redeem time. This means God can reinstate or bring back time that has been lost. God can add, subtract, multiply and divide time as He pleases. God can make the most of every opportunity that would have been lost within the restraints of time. Eph.1:10 (EXB) talks about the **fullness of time,** when all things come properly into place for fulfillment of His plan. God does not delay and is not slow or late about His promises, but "He is extraordinarily patient toward us, not desiring that any should perish". (**2Pet.3:9 AMP**) God always brings things to pass **just in time**… never too early, never too late.

THE RIGHT TIME

Ecc.3:1-3 says, there is a season or **an appointed time** for everything. We have to adapt ourselves to the times of life. What time is it in your life? Is it a time in your life to plant yourself or be planted by God in a particular work or ministry? Is it time for some things within ourselves or our ministries to be rooted out or plucked up? What is it in our lives or spirits that we need to kill or mortify? What wounds or hurts within us can the Holy Spirit cause to heal at this time? What needs to be broken down, and what needs to be built up? But is it the right time? The right time is the time that is acceptable or approved by God.

THE FRUSTRATION OF TIME

Waiting on time can be frustrating. How many of us get frustrated while waiting on time for an anticipated event to happen? If we're not mindful to be willing to patiently wait on God's perfect timing, we can experience all types of emotions during the wait. These can include fear, anger, boredom, depression, stepping back (in faith, work, giving etc.). They could also include anxiety, discouragement, worry, impatience, and even the temptation to jump ahead of God's timing. Probably all of us can relate to having experienced at least some of these emotions.

Going forward from here, let's remind ourselves how finite our minds are and how much higher God's ways are than ours. God's time is the perfect time, and deep down inside, we wouldn't want to have it any other way.

HOLY SPIRIT WILL HELP

From now on, let us flow with God's timing to obtain His blessings for our lives. If we pray, Holy Spirit will even help us, encourage us, and direct our attention toward other activities until the time is right for that particular move.

So let us joyfully wait for God to say, "**Its time**". Then we know that we will have the best opportunity to have the highest blessing and be the most pleasing to God.

This is maximizing God's timing and His plans for us. Much fruit can be yielded when it is planted, watered, and cultivated in its season. The fruit that is produced is lush and sweet and many can be blessed by it.

Good seed for the best fruit must be planted in planting season, cultivated in its season for cultivation and harvested at its harvest time.

GOD'S Timing is Everything!

70

I AM SOMEBODY

I AM SOMEBODY GOD LOVES

God loves me with an everlasting love. With His loving kindness He draws me to Himself and continues His faithfulness towards me. God planned for me to be His own before He formed the foundations of the world. God's love for me is unconditional, not dependent upon anything that I do. God sacrificed the life of His Son, Jesus, to save me from Hell and to redeem me from sin so that I could have eternal life with Him. Christ volunteered to die on the cross, in my place, as payment for my sin debt. By this I know that the Almighty, all-knowing sovereign God believes I AM SOMEBODY who is worthy of His love.

I AM SOMBODY ACCEPTED BY GOD

I am so glad that my worth is not defined by man's criteria or judgement. It doesn't matter if I never get acknowledgement or accolades from anyone. The Bible said I am "accepted" in Jesus (the Beloved). God's thoughts concerning me are perpetually "good". I am somebody because God has said so.

I AM SOMEBODY CREATED IN GOD'S IMAGE

God made me a little lower than the angels. I didn't make myself. I am created in the image and likeness of the creator of this universe. What higher credentials are there? I am to **show forth His glory and image forth His ways and let the same mind that Christ has be also in me.** This is my goal so that I may win the prize of the "high calling of God in Christ Jesus", and I press toward it.

I AM SOMBODY GOD PREFERS

God shows His favor towards me by giving me preferential treatment. I AM SOMEBODY who is a part of God's family, part of His Body, and a joint-heir with Christ, His Son. God made provisions for me to receive all the benefits He desired for me to have. He inspired men to write down in sixty-six books, step by step, point by point, instructions for me to follow. In them are His inspired words that contain all truth, wisdom and knowledge to equip me to live a victorious life. Although His favor Is unmerited, He does these things because He loves me, and I am His friend. He has invested in me and entrusted me to fulfill His Kingdom purposes.

I AM SOMEBODY ON GOD'S MIND

God's mind is full of thoughts of me. I matter to God. God knows me by my name. Before I was born, He knew me. I am the apple of His eye. His eye is always on me. God wrote in a book all the days of my life before I ever lived one of them. He knows me inside and out. He sees me as yet becoming who He made me to be. I bare all before Him. There is nothing that is hidden. Still nothing hinders His love for me. I AM SOMEBODY because He made me to be. I am His workmanship. I was created in Christ to do the good works which He prepared in advance for me to do. I am His ambassador. I am an extension of Him. I become His arms, legs, feet and mouth to spread His Word and compel men to be reconciled to Him. By the Holy Spirit, God empowers me to do these things. There is no doubt that I AM SOMEBODY.

I AM SOMEBODY WHO LOVES GOD

I am God's servant. I will serve Him with gladness until I die. I want Him to fulfill His calling on my life and accomplish what pleases Him. I love and adore Him. I am a true worshipper because I worship Him in spirit and in truth. As He has sought such, He has found in me. **I AM SOMEBODY.**

71

GOOD EXPECTATIONS

GOOD GIFTS

Never give up on anyone. Encourage them not to give up on themselves and not to give up on God. God has given to each one of us good gifts: talents, abilities, physical and even spiritual strength.

Demonstrate, by your words and actions, your belief in God's Word as found in **Jer. 29:11 KJV** which says, "**For I know the thoughts that I think toward you, saith the Lord, thoughts of peace, and not of evil, to give an expected end**." God has plans for our welfare to give us a future. We must seek Him with our whole heart. Stand strong in our faith in Him "for He is faithful that promised". (**Heb. 10:23 KJV**)

GOOD POTENTIAL

Good expectations can be seen as good potential. God has put into each of us the potential to accomplish great things. Having potential means having the power which comes from the Holy Spirit. "For it is God who works in you to will and to act in order to fulfill **His good purpose**. (**Eph. 2:13 NIV**)

Just as God has good expectations for us, we are to have good expectations for one another. We are to see one another as a child who is fearfully and wonderfully made by God. We cannot underestimate what God is able to do with His children, for He "is able to do exceeding abundantly above all that we ask or think according to the power that worketh in us." (**Eph.3:20 KJV**) The power that is working in us is Holy Ghost power. There is nothing too hard for us because there is nothing too hard for Him.

GOOD INTENTIONS

We should have good expectations and good intentions for the family of believers. We should afford them every benefit of the doubt. We should follow the leading of the Holy Ghost before we form negative opinions. We must look beyond what we see, and instead see what God sees in them. Think positively about them and about ourselves also. It is God who we are to look to. It is His opinion that counts. God hates the sin, not the sinner. God knows everything. He will never leave us nor forsake us. He will equip us to achieve those desires that He has placed in our hearts.

GOOD FUTURE

Encourage one another to move forward and not backwards. God has their back and front. They need to move forward in faith and integrity (meaning honesty). They need to follow the leading of the Holy Ghost, having their steps ordered by God. Encourage them to move forward without fear. Even if they stumble, the Lord will hold their hand, stand them back up and give them a firm footing. So tell them to go forward, adhering to His Word, trust and believe He will do whatever He has promised. Speak in agreement with His Words, for they are spirit and they are life. It is the Spirit that quickens, gives life. Holy Spirit will help you to move forward to accomplish the purposes of God. Encourage one another to "stay the course". Do the work. Walk the narrow path. Resist being seduced by the lust of the eyes, the lust of the flesh, and the pride of life.

Believe that there are **good things** in store for us. I exhort you to walk by faith and not by sight. Without faith it is impossible to please God. Worship and praise God daily. Pray for one another. Pray in agreement with God's good expectations for us. Use His Word to come against the enemy. Apply the blood of Jesus to your circumstances. Use God's Word to fight for one another. Wage spiritual warfare on behalf of one another. Stand in the gap for the ones who can't fight for themselves.

72

THE WORKING
OF MIRACLES

COVET EARNESTLY THE BEST GIFTS

After Paul listed the nine gifts of the Spirit shown in 1Cor.12, he went on to say, "**But covet earnestly the best gifts.** <u>To covet means to eagerly desire, be zealous for.</u> **The best gift is the gift needed at that time.** Under certain circumstances, even the very best gift of all the spiritual gifts may not be the best gift in a given circumstance or the gift needed at that particular time.

THE WORKING OF MIRACLES DEFINED

A miracle can be defined as a supernatural intervention by God in the ordinary course of nature.

As with many words in the English language, when we use the word "**miracle**" generally speaking, it means one thing; but used specifically, it means something else. **For example,** sometimes the word "**miracle**" is used generally as a figure of speech. We talk, for instance, about <u>miracle</u> fabrics, <u>miracle</u> drugs, <u>miracle</u> detergents, and so forth.

In nature we might see a beautiful sunrise and say, "That's a **miracle**". We might look at a beautiful rose garden ablaze with glorious color, the perfume of the flowers ascending into the heavens, and say that it is a "**miracle**" of nature.

None of these things are a miracle specifically speaking, because they are doing exactly what they ought to do according to the laws of nature. Remember that **a miracle is a supernatural intervention by God in the ordinary course of nature.**

Generally speaking, <u>all Gifts of the Spirit</u> are <u>miracles</u>, but *specifically* speaking, all of them are not. When the Working of Miracles is in manifestation**, there is a divine intervention in the ordinary course of nature.**

Everything that God does is miraculous in a sense, but specifically, turning common dust into insects just by a gesture is a miracle and turning common water into wine just by speaking a word is a miracle. These two occurrences are <u>examples of</u> **Working of Miracles.**

A more detailed definition of the Gift of Working of Miracles is a supernatural intervention in the ordinary course of nature, a temporary suspension of the accustomed order, or an interruption in the system of nature as we know it, operated by the power of the Holy Spirit.

NEW TESTAMENT EXAMPLES OF WORKING OF MIRACLES

For provision

- Jesus took the little boy's lunch and fed 5,000 with it.

To carry out divine judgement:

- Ananias and Sapphira fell dead after lying to the Holy Ghost

To confirm the preached word:

- When Paul was preaching in Cyprus, Elymas the sorcerer tried to stop the Governor from believing in Jesus. Elymas was struck blind for a season.

However, the **Working of Miracles** could also be included where it says in **Acts 5:12 KJV**, "And by the hands of the Apostles were many SIGNS AND WONDERS wrought among the people". There are other passages in the New Testament where the **Working of Miracles** is also directly mentioned. For examples, see reference pages.

When the Lord permits a person through the power of the Holy Spirit to speak a word, and the miraculous occurs, then the same God who created the world is allowing some of His omnipotence to be manifested (by extension) through that person.

73

PERPETUAL CHANGE

A MUST

Perpetual means continuing forever. What we are saying today is <u>nothing continues forever except change.</u> Everything **must** change. From the face of this earth to the faces of its inhabitants, everything must change. Nothing stays the same. It is not possible for change not to take place because that is the way God planned it. Job said, … I will wait till my change comes. **Psalms 30:5 KJV** says. "…weeping may endure for a night, but joy cometh in the morning." Knowing that change is coming should give us all something to look forward to, something to be at peace with.

A PART OF LIFE

Seasons change. People change. Circumstances change. We live, we impact the earth and its inhabitants in some way, and then we die. It is the cycle of life. Time changes things, and age changes things. God changes things as He wills.

There will always be movement because nothing is stagnant. Some movement happens too fast to see, for example, the rotation of the earth. Some movement happens so slowly it is barely detectable. You can barely see it, for example, some bugs or some plants.

Don't expect things not to move in the spirit realm as well. Only God does not change. He is the same yesterday and today and **forever**.

CHANGING TO LIVE

In God's wisdom, He made our bodies to function so that our cells are continuously replenishing and reproducing themselves so that our lives are sustained. Because of the plan of God, there will be constant evolving, changing and recycling of the process of life. So, change is **necessary for life**.

Sometimes change may be feared, but change is inevitable. Nothing is permanent except God and His Word.

ACCORDING TO HIS PURPOSE

We can have the confidence to know that we will be alright because God will work everything out for our good. **God has purpose for change**. We need to embrace that truth. Without change, His purpose cannot take place. Never get too complacent with the present state of things because lack of change is equal to stagnation, which is death (spiritual and natural). Be ready to adapt to change. We can make some changes on our own, but the outcome is up to God.

PRESCRIBED CHANGE

God **prescribes** specific changes for us in our individual daily circumstances, things that we would not ordinarily predict would happen. These changes are unexpected turns of events. These changes may be big or small interventions on our behalf that serve to protect us, encourage us or grow us. They also remind us of God's love for us and His sovereignty. He does not have to follow the world's expectations.

WELCOME CHANGE

Some change is welcomed and anticipated, especially when we see a need for it, for example, healing, deliverance or advancement toward a goal.

God put change into motion at creation. And it was so. God upholds, propels and continues the perpetual changing and movement of the universe to this day by the Word of His power.

74

HE CARRIES US

FROM THE SITUATION

Have you ever been brought through or brought out of a troubling situation and cannot explain how? It may have felt like going to sleep at point A and waking up at point B not being able to explain how you got there. However, you know that it wasn't because of any magic wand that you or any particular person had that caused you to land safely at point B. In certain passages of scripture, Jesus went (passed) through a crowd (a situation) unseen. **John 8:59 KJV** says, "He hid Himself...going through the midst of them..." Also, in John 12:36, Jesus hid Himself from His disciples. Jesus will hide us under His wings and will shield and protect us.

HIDE ME

Often in the midst of a storm or just an on-coming danger, Jesus will **carry** us through unharmed and unscathed, and sometimes without any negative effect on us at all. It's like we are temporarily removed from the situation and taken to another place although we are still living through it until it has passed. We can be **in** the situation, yet mentally, spiritually and even physically **removed** from it. Some people may not have yet had such an experience, but for sure, some have. "For in the time of trouble, He shall **hide me** in His pavilion, in the secret of His tabernacle shall He hide me; He shall set me up upon a rock." (**Ps. 27:5 KJV**)

We don't have to look like what we've been through, and God can still make a good outcome of it. **Is. 43:2 KJV** says, "when thou passeth through the waters, I will be with thee; and through the rivers, they shall not overflow thee: when thou walkest through the fire, thou shalt not be burned; neither shall the flames kindle upon thee."

ON EAGLES WINGS

God lifts us up over our circumstances and places us on a firm safe ground. God said in **Isaiah 46:4 KJV, "I will carry you.** I have made you, and I will carry and will save you". (AMP) It is just as when God delivered the Israelites out of Egypt in such a miraculous way that there was no doubt that He carried them out, although they were being chased by Pharaoh's army. God said in **Exodus 19:4 EXB, "I carried you** out of Egypt, as if on eagles' wings, and I brought you here to me." **Ps.19:11-12 EXB** says that His angels **will bear (lift) us up** in their hands to keep us safe. God will carry us.

OUR DELIVERER

Whatever situation we may be faced with, let us cast all of our cares upon the Lord. Tell Him all about it. He cares about us. He takes care of us. By prayer and supplication, let your request be made known unto God, and the peace of God will guard your hearts and minds through Christ Jesus. He will give us peace in the midst of trouble. You will not lose your mind because He will post a guard around it.

"Trust in the Lord with all your heart. Lean not (don't depend) on your own understanding..." (**Pro. 3:5-6 KJV**) You don't have the capacity to comprehend what God has in His mind for you, how He wants to bless and deliver you. So, just acknowledge Him (honor Him) with prayer, obedience, praise and worship, and let Him direct your path to safety and full deliverance. Don't be afraid. Stand still and you will see the salvation of the Lord. God encourages and assures us that with His mighty hand of power, He will help us, strengthen us and hold us until we are able to stand.

75

YOU CAN DEPEND ON GOD

ASSURANCE

Do you know that you can depend on God? You have probably heard it and may have even said it, but do you really know it for yourself? God is a covenant keeping God, a promise keeper. If He has said it, He will do it. He is not slack nor does He tire. If you will take Him at His Word, you will know that He has sworn by His own un-erring, all-powerful sovereignty that He will never fail us or let us down. Heb.13:5 AMP tells us that we don't need to worry about or crave after anything. For He shall supply all our need according to His riches in glory by Christ Jesus, and "… no good thing will He withhold from them that walk uprightly." (**Ps.84:11 KJV**)

God gives us even more assurance in **Heb.13:5AMP** where He said, "I will not in any way fail you **nor** give you up **nor** leave you without support. And then He repeats, "I will not, I will not in any degree leave you helpless nor forsake nor let you down (relax my hold on you)! **Assuredly not!**"

HIS INTENTIONS

It is God's intention that we be blessed.) It was always His purpose. He always had good plans for us. Even **Rom. 8:28 KJV** says that "all things work together for our good to those who love Him and are "the called" according to His purpose". We are "the called". God commands us to love Him with all our hearts, all our souls, all our minds and all our strength. We are to have no other God before Him for He is a jealous God.

GOD'S LOVE FOR US

For God so loved us that He sacrificed His Son, Jesus Christ to save us from our sins. In Isaiah 41:10, God tells us that we can lean on Him and count on Him for support. Numb.21:3 says that God cannot lie, and John 17:17 says that His Word is "TRUTH". We have an open invitation to come into His presence of in prayer to receive mercy and grace to help in the time of need.

TRUST GOD

Pro.3:5-6 KJV says, "Trust in the Lord with all thine heart and lean not unto thine own understanding." In all thy ways acknowledge (honor, ask) Him, and He shall direct thy path. "Do not have anxiety about anything, but in every circumstance and in everything, by prayer and petition (definite requests), with thanksgiving, continue to make your wants known to God." (**Phil.4:6 AMP**) Make a commitment to follow the Lord's ways. Don't get upset or be angry. Rest in your confidence in the Lord.

ALWAYS DEPEND

Depend on God daily, not just in difficult circumstances or in lack, but throughout every day. We can depend on Him to direct our paths. We will be rewarded if we diligently seek Him for direction. God has given us the Holy Spirit to guide us into all truth, but we need to inquire, listen and obey in faith.

God will not always show us the outcome of our obedience initially, but as we move in the confidence that He's working everything out for our good, at the end, God will reveal to us the blessed rewards of our obedience and trust. We can depend on God to do whatever He has promised.

76

OUTFITTED FOR
HIS PURPOSE

ORDAINED

According to Eph. 2:10AMP when we were created, <u>God had already</u> **ordained** <u>us</u> for a purpose and a plan and prepared beforehand the paths that we should walk to live out His plan. Ordained means <u>to be appointed</u> <u>to a position of authority with specific abilities</u>. Not only has God given us the ability **to become the sons of God.** God also gave us all things that we would need to fulfill His excellent purpose. We are well equipped and well able to perform His good work. We are **thoroughly furnished and appropriately prepared** for the tasks that lie ahead.

BEING PREPARED

If you were taking a trip and had to pack a bag, what you would pack would depend on if you were packing for a vacation or for a business trip. If you accidentally brought the wrong bag, you would find yourself unprepared for the designated activities. In Christ, there is a job or specific activity that we, as believers, are designed for. We were all called **to reconcile people back to a right relationship with God.** Now we have **the Holy Spirit** to teach us and empower us for this ministry work.

SPECIALIZED WORK

Before we were born, God planned a package **of special experiences** we would need in order for Him to **outfit** us for certain designated tasks. God has chosen and fitted us with certain experiences that would build in us the kind of strength of character that we would need for this specialized work. Only God knew what kinds of experiences these would be. And step by step, God has brought and still is bringing us through these life experiences. We may not understand why God has deemed certain experiences necessary, but we must fully trust that he does everything for our good and for His purpose.

FOR THE SOVEREIGN GOD

It is God's decision what He allows or fixes for us to go through. How will we respond to His sovereignty? Will we respond with anger and self-pity? Poor me, Why me? Will you condemn God? God this isn't fair. Will you lose your joy and just be head-bowed and down-trodden? Will you be confused or become afraid? Will you become desperate enough to seek comfort outside of God and His will? Will you be sad and depressed? Will you be disappointed that God didn't follow your plan or your desire? Will you be unable to give God praise or to worship Him in spirit and in truth? There will be ups and downs, some good times and some bad times. But remember who is ultimately in charge. Put your full trust in God, no matter the circumstances.

DISTRACTIONS

Don't be distracted by life's experiences. Remember, God has purpose for everything. We can either use our free will and faith to submit to

God's plan or rebel against it. Either way God's plan will go forward. His specialized work will just be done by someone else, and we will miss out on His blessings that He had planned for us. Let nothing distract or separate us from the love of Christ, for we are more than conquerors through Him that loved us.

REFERENCES FOR FURTHER STUDY

Title #s

1. Mark 11:17, Is.43:7, John 4:23, 2Cor.10:5, Rom.12:1
2. James 1:4, Ex.9:1, Joshua 24:15, Ex.34:14, Joshua 24:20, John 10:10
3. 2Chron.20:6, Jer.1:12, Deut.28:15, Pro.3:5-6, Eph.3:20, Jer.29:11, Rom.8:28, John 11:4, Jer.31:3, Ps.139:1-3, Ps.31:15, Is.44:6, Rev.1:8, Ps.90:2, Heb.13:5, Gen.18:14, Rom.8:31, Hos.13:4,
4. Dan.5:27, Gal.5:1, Ps.1:1-2, 2Pet.1:4-7, Gal.5:22-23
5. Eph.4:11-13, Phil.3:21, 1Thes.4:17, 2Cor.3:18, Rom.8:29, 2Tim.3:17, James 1:4, 2Pet.1:3, Ps.100:3, Jer.17:9, Eph.5:27, Matt.5:16,
6. Pro.29:18 AMP, NLV, NLT, Gen.22:13-14 AMP, Matt.6:10, Matt.16:16, Heb.7:25, Gen.6:14-16,
7. 2Cor.2:14, 1Cor. 15:57, Heb.13:5 AMP, Rom. 8:28, Jer. 29:11
8. Gen.50:20, Matt.14:16-21, Mark 16:6, Heb.1:3, Pro.3:5-6, Matt.14:16-21, Mark 9:23
9. Ps.139:7-9, Gen.1:3-10, Rev.4:8, Jer.29:11. Deut.26:15, Jer.29:11, Pro.3:5-6, Ps.119:133, Gen.16:13, Is.46:10, 3John 1:2, Acts 4:27-28 EXB, Rom.8:28

10. 1Pet.4:13, Titus 1:2, Jer.1:12 AMP, 1John 5:14-15, Ps.121:1-2, Ps.91:15, 2Cor.1:20, James 1:7, John 3:16, 1Pet.5:7, Ps.27:14, Eph.6:11, Heb.10:36, Ps.37:7, Lam.3:23, Ps.34:19, Ps.27:1, Ps.3:3, Is.61:3 MSG, Phil.4:6-7, 1Pet.5:10, Job 14:14, Ps.84:11, James 2:14, Luke 19:13

11. Eph.4:12, Matt.5:3-11, Luke 2:49, Luke4:18, Phil.2:12, 2Cor.5:18

12. Is.41:10, Rom.5:8, 1Pet.1:16, 1John 1:9, Ps.103:112, Ps.107:1, Heb.13:5, Deut.7:8, Ps.46:1, Heb.13:8, 1John 3:1, Eph.1:5, 1John 1:12, Eph.1:5, Eph.2:4-6, John 14:2-3, Heb.10:5,7, Is.53:5, Mark 16:6, Heb.7:25, John 15:13

13. Gal.5:22, 1Tim.2:9, Eph.4:29, 2Cor.5:17, Col.3:2, Ps.103:2, Gen.6:5, 2Cor.10:5, Jer.29:11, Ps.40:8, Deut.28::1-14, 2Tim.3:16-17,

14. Matt.25:21, Eph.6:12-17, 1Cor.15:58, Col.1:23, Phil.2:12, Jude 1:20, 2Pet.1:5-7, Is.50:7, Ps.91:1AMP, Ps.16:11, 1Chron.4:10, John 15:16

15. Amos 3:3, Eph.4:13, Eph.1:22-23, Rom.12:5, 1Cor.14:10, 2Pet.1:4, 2Pet.1:8 MSG, John 4:12, 1Cor.2:16, 1Thes.5:23-24, John 14:26, John 17:21

16. Rev.1:10-20, Acts 9:10-12, 1Sam.9:3-20, 1Sam.10:21-23, 2Kings 5:21-26, 2Kings 6:11-12, 1Kings 19:14

17. 1Kings 18:41, 1Kings 18:39, Eph.3:20, 1Kings 18:42, Matt.11:29-30 AMP, 1Kings 18:41, Job 14:14, Job 42:10, Hab.2:3, 1Kings 18:43-45 AMP, 2Pet.3:8, 1Pet.5:10, Phil.3:12-14,

18. Ps.100:3, Rom.8:28, 2Tim.1:9, Eph.1:5, Jer.29:11, Eph.1:4-6 AMP, 1Cor.8:3 AMP, Luke 12:2-3, Job 34:21, Ps.139:14 NLT, Ps.139:2-3,16 AMP, Jer.29:11, Eph.1:5, Heb.13:21 AMP, Rom.8:29-30 AMP, 1Pet.1:6-7 AMP, James 1:2-4, Ps.34:19, 1Thes.5:24

19. 1Pet.1:16, John 17:17, Rom.12:18, 1John 3:4, Ex.26:33-34, Heb.12:14, 1John 1:5-6, Ps.24:3-4, Rom.8:5 AMP, Gal.5:25, Gal.5:22-23, Gal.5:16 AMP, 1Pet.1:23 AMP

20. John 8:32, John 14:6, Gal.5:1, John 8:36, Rom.7:19, Rom.6:13, 1Cor.9:27, Rom.6:6, Rom.5:2, Gal.5:17, Rom.7:21,23, Eph.6:11, 2Cor.10:4, 1John 2:14, Col.3:16, Matt.4:4, Deut.30:14 AMP, Pro.23:7, Luke 10:27, Matt.37:40, 2Pet.1:3

21. Matt.5:16, 2Cor.3:2, John 1:14, Phil.1:7, John 14:6, 2Tim.3:16-17MSG, Heb.4:12 AMP, John 6:63, Gal.5:22-23

22. John 14:16-17, Eph.1:20-21, 2Kings 6:16, Matt.28:20, Phil.4:6-7,1Pet.5:10, Heb.4:16, Ps.91:11, 1Pet.5:7

23. 1Tim.6:5,9-11 AMP, Ecc.10:19: Life Appl., 1Tim.6:8, Phil.4:11-12 AMP, Matt.6:32, Deut.8:18, 1Tim.6:17, -19, Matt.6:24 MSG, Eph.3:20

24. 1Pet.2:9, Ps.119:130, 2Cor.4:1, 2Cor.4:4, Gen.2:7, Acts 1:8, 2Cor.5:20, 2Cor.5:17, 2Cor.4:1, 1Pet.5:6, Jer.18:4

25. 1Cor.4:7, Matt.22:21

26. Rev.4:9-10, Rev.1:10, Ps.34:1, Rev,1:10, John 4:24, Ps.34:1, 2Cor.10:5, Heb.13:15

27. Rom.8:23 AMP, 2Cor.5:17, John 3:7, John 1:13 AMP, Eph.2:5, Eph.2:10, 1Thes.1:9, Col.3:4, John1:3-4, 2Pet.1:3, Rom.1:6, 2Pet.1:4,10, 2Pet.1:4, Phil.1:21, 2Cor.5:8, Phil.3:21, Heb.9:28, Heb.2:15, 1Cor.15:26

28. John 1:12-13, Jer.31:3, 2Pet.1:3, Rom.8:17 AMP, Matt.3:17, Luke 2:40 AMP, Heb.4:16, Ps.16:3, Deut.32:10, Ps.8:4, Eph.4:30 AMP, Rom.8:16, John 14:17, 1Cor.6:19-20, Rom.8:15 AMP, 1John3:1 AMP, John 14:17, Ps.100:3, Is.43:7

29. Pro.3:1-2,5, Heb.11:6, Rom.8:28, Rom.8:13, James1:6-7, Heb.6:13, Jer.1:12, Ps/89:34, 2Cor.1:20, Deut.28:45-58

30. Col.2:9, Heb.12:2, 2Tim.3:16-17, Is.26:3 AMP, Pro.3:5-6, 1Thes.5:24, Heb.1:3, Gen.1:1, Luke 10:19, Heb.9:27-28, John 19:30

31. Gen.17:1, Matt.28:18, 1Cor.2:4-5, John 11:40-45, Ps.27:2, Dan.6:22,26-27, Is.41:10, Dan.3:16-17,29, Pro.3:5-6, 2Cor.1:20, 1Pet.5:7, Heb.4:16, Joshua 1:9, Heb.13:5, Rev.3:7

32. Heb.5:12-13, Heb.5:1 MSG, 1Cor.9:24, Col.3:2, Heb.5:14, 1John 4:6

33. Matt.18:14, Heb.10:5, 1Pet.2:24, Matt.27:51-52, John 2:19, Rom.6:14, Heb.2:15, Rom.8:11, 1Cor.6:14, 1Cor.15:57, Luke 10:19, Rom.6:11 AMP, Rom.8:37, 2Cor.2:14, Rom.8:1-4, Is.59:19, Job 23:10, Ps.66:10, 2Cor,4:16, Jer.18:3-4

34. Rom.12:1-2 AMP, 1Cor.3:7, John 14:15, Gal.5:22-23, Mark 7:25-30, Luke 8:43-48, John 4:23, 29,39, John 12:32, Ps.91:1-11, Ps.103:1-3

35. Rom.1:21-28, Rom.6:13,16-18, John 2:16, Pro.4:23, Rom.12:1, Gal.2:20, Matt.6:10, John13:13-16, Jer.29:11, Haggai 1:5

36. John 14:17, 26, John 16:13 AMP, 1Cor.2:11, 1Cor.2:10,12 AMP, Eph.4:11, Is.11:2

37. Rom.1:19-20 AMP, Ps.115:4-7, Ez.28:15,17, Gen.3:1,6, Is.14:14, 1Pet.5:8, 2Cor.5:20, 1John 4:17, John 3:16, 2Pet.1:4, 1John 4:7, John 1:33

38. John 16:33, Is.26:3 AMP, 2Cor.12:10, 1Cor.2:14, Phil.4:9

39. Acts 5:42 AMP, Matt.16:13-19, 2Cor.4:4, Matt.16:18, Luke 11:2, Luke 4:41

40. John 6:63, Col.3:4, 1Pet.2:9, John1:9, Ps.119:105, John17:17, Rom.10:8-10, Ps.22:3, John1:14, John 6:63, 2Tim.3:15, Pro.2:6, Pro.4:7 AMP, John 1:1

41. Phil.4:7, Pro.4:23, Eph.4:27, 2Cor.10:5, Matt.4:1-11, James 4:7, John 14:27, Neh.8:10, Ex.12:7, 1Cor.2:16, 1Cor.6:19-20, Gal.5:1, 1Cor.14:33, Phil.4:8, Phil.2:15

42. Eph.1:1-4, John 10:10, 1John 1:7, Matt.16:19 AMP, 2Cor.10:4-5, Phil.2:10, Rom.8:28, Zech.2:8, Jer.29:11, Eph.1:4-5, Eph.1:6, Jer.31:3

43. Ps.139:7-12, Ez.48:35, Ezek.48:35, Ps.46:1, Gen.17:1, John 5:26-27 AMP, Ps.31:15, John 1:3, Gen.1:3-31, Ps.24:1, Gen.1:1, 1Cor.8:6, Heb.1:2-3 AMP, Is.46:11, Is.64:8, Is.46:10, Jer.18:4, Rev.21:2-3, Gen.1:2, John 1:1 AMP, Col.2:10, Phil.2:9-11, Rev.20:11-15, Rev.22:13, Rev.1:1-2

44. Rom.10:9, John 3:7, 1Cor.5:17, Rom.8:16, Heb.10:25, 2Tim.3:17, Matt.15:8, 2Tim.3:16-17, John 4:23-24, Phil.3:12, Rom.5:9 AMP, Ps.139:21-22, Phil.3:10 AMP

45. Ex.6:3 AMP, Pro.16:7, John 16:33, Ex.4:2, Eph.4:3 AMP, Ps.118:23, Ex.7:8-10, Eph.1:17-19 AMP, Ex.4:11, Pro.3:5

46. Phil.4:6-7 AMP, Heb.11:6, Rev.8:4 AMP, Deut.9:24-26, Pro.3:5-6, 1Cor.14:14-15, Jude 20, Luke 18:1, Rom.8:26, James 5:16, Phil.4:6, Mark 11:24, 1Pet.1:13 AMP, 1Pet.1:13 AMP, Col.3:16, John 14:26, John 16:23-24, 1Thes.5:18, Matt.21:21-22, Phil.4:6,Acts

13:2, Acts 4:24, 2Chron.5:11-14 AMP, Ezek.22:30, Matt.18:19-20, 1Pet.5:8, Eph.6:11, 2Cor.10:4

47. Matt.19:17, James 1:22, 2Cor.5:21, Rom.14:12, Luke 6:42 AMP, 2Cor.5:20, Mark 12:30, Ex.20:3, John 1:29, Heb.10:12 AMP, 1Pet.1:15, Rom.8:38-39, Jer.31:3, Rev.2:19-20, Acts 3:19 AMP, Dan.5:27, 1John 1:9, Matt.6:34 AMP

48. 2Pet.1:7 EXB, 2Tim.1:7, Eph.1:5 AMP, John 13:34, John 3:16, Matt.22:39, 1John 3:17-18 AMP, Gal.5:22 AMP, John 10:10, Is.41:10, Jer.31:3 AMP, Phil.2:3-4, 1Cor.13:4-8, Matt.7:21-23, Rom.5:5

49. 2Tim.3:16, Pro.1:25, 1Cor.9:27, Rom.6:14, James 3:15-16 AMP, Gen.1:27-28,31 AMP, Gen.1:4 AMP, Luke 7:30 EXB, Col.3:5-6, Lev.18:1-30, James 1:13-14 AMP, 2Tim.3:16

50. James 3:16

51. Heb.12:2, 2Chron.16:9 EXB, Rom.8:28, Ps.116:2, Mark 11:24, James 5:16, 1John 5:14, Deut.8:13-14, Ps.118:5, Luke 22:33, Eph.3:20, Is.40:28 EXB, Is.55:9, 1Cor.15:57-58, Ps.37:1-5 John 15:5, Gen.22:13-14, Ex.15:26, Ex.17:15, Lev.20:8, Gal.3:13, Eph.2:8, 1Cor.15:57, Ez.48:35, 1Cor.1:29, Ps.118:23

52. John 17:21 AMP, 1John 5:7, Matt. 19:17 AMP, 1John5:6 AMP, 1John 4:8, Matt.28:18, Matt.6:9 EXB, Mark 1:24 AMP, John 14:16-17 EXB, 1John 5:7, Eph.1:11 AMP, Ps.96:4 AMP, John 5:30, 37;15:26, John 14:6,9, Ps.150:2-6, Ps.145:3, Ps.62:11

53. Col.1:27, Col.2:9-10, John 17:21, 2Cor.4:17 AMP, Ps.9:2, John 3:16, Eph.3:20, Phil.2:13, Phil.4:13, Matt.11:30, Neh.8:10, 2Cor.5:20, 1Tim.6:12-14, Rom. 12:1, John 15:5, Pro.4:23, Eph.4:3 AMP, Heb.1:3, 1Chron.16:29, 2Chron.5:13-14, 1Eph.1:18 AMP, Eph.4:6, Phil.4:13 AMP, Eph.1:3, 2Pet.1:3

54. John 14:18, Luke 11:13, Matt.3:11, Luke 24:49, Acts 1:8, Rom.6:8, John 14:26, John 13:13, Acts 2:4, Acts 13:2, Acts 16:6, 2Cor.3:6, Rom.8:9, 1Cor.6:19, Titus 3:5, John 3:3, Acts 13:2,

55. Mark 16:18, 2Pet.1:1, Ps.133:3, Heb.4:16, 2Cor.4:13-15, Rom.10:9-10, Matt.9:24,

56. Is.55:11, 2Tim.3:16, Ps.33:6, 2Sam.22:29, John 1:14 AMP, Gal.2:20

57. Ps.111:60, Ps.119:7-10, Gen.22:13-14, 2Cor.1:20, Rom.8:28, James 1:6-7, Ps.68:19, Matt.6:34, Col.3:2
58. Matt.19:4-6, 1Cor.12:12, Eph.5:23, 2Cor.11:12, Rev.21:9, Jer.34:18, Gal.2:20, Eph.5:26-27, 1Pet.1:2-5
59. Phil.4:18, Matt.6:32, Matt.22:37,39, James 1:27, 2Cor,3:5, John 15:5, 2Cor.9:8, Phil.4:11, 2Cor.12:9, Ps.23:1 AMP, Is.41:10, Heb.13:5, Ps.91:11, 2Cor.2:14, 1Sam.21:49-50, Gen.17:1, Ex.3:14
60. 2Pet.3:9, John 3:16, Heb.4:16, Mark 1:17, Matt. 14:29, Matt.11:28, John 10:27, Jer.29:11, Rom.8:28, Gen.7:1, Pro.18:10, Num.10:29, Rom.10:13, Rev.22:17, Is.55:1, Matt.22:4-6, John 14:2, John 10:28
61. Gal.6:10 AMP, Eph.4:2, Eph.4:16, 2Pet.1:1,3-4 AMP, 2Pet.1:3, 2Pet.1:4 AMP, Mk.3:33-35, 1John 4:1, John 8:47 AMP
62. 2Tim.1:7, Rom.5:2, Gen.22:14, Ex.15:26, Is.59:19, Ps.3:3, Jer.31:3, Ps.17:8, Ps.8:4, Jer.29:11
63. Ps.24:1, 1Chron.29:12, Ps.100:3, Is.29:16, Is.55:9, Ps.31:15, Matt.13:23, Job 38:11, 31-33, Mark 4:39, Is.40:22-24 Amp
64. Matt.6:13, Col.2:15, Ps.98:1, Ps.119:133, Deut.30:19, James 1:15, John 10:10, Phil.3:18-19 AMP
65. Matt.4:4, Jer.29:11
66. Heb.11:6, Heb.13:15, Col.1:16-17, 2Cor.1:20, Luke 1:37, Lam.3:22-23, 2Cor.10:5
67. Matt.15:11, James 3:6 NIV, Deut.30:19, Mark 11:23, James 3:6 MSG, James 3:9 AMP, James 3:18 AMP, Pro.3:5-6, John 6:63
68. Eph.1:4-5, Rev.1:8, Gen.1:11-31, John 8:12, Ecc.12:7, Ecc.3:2, John 12:25, Gen.2:7, Jer.29:11, Joshua 24:15, Deut.30:19, John 14:6, Col.3:4, Eph.2:3 AMP, Gal.5:1 AMP
69. Amos 8:9, Eph.5:16 NIV, Eph.1:10 EXB, 2Pet.3:8 EXB, Ecc.3:1-3, Rom.8:13, Luke 4:19, Is.55:8-9
70. Jer.31:3, Eph.1:4, Heb.10:7, Eph.1:6, Jer.29:11, Deut.28:13, Ps.8:5, Ps.103:3, Gen.1:27, Phil.2:5, Phil.3:14, Rom.8:17, 2Tim.3:16, Ps.119:133, John 15:15, 2Pet.1:3-4, Ps.8:4, Ex.33:12, Jer.1:5, Ps.17:8, Ps.139:16, Gen.16:13, Ps.69:5, Ps.133:114, Eph.2:10, 2Cor.5:20, Acts 1:8, Heb.2:7b, Ps.100:2, Is.55:11, John 4:23
71. James 1:17, Ps.119:2, Ps.139:14, Acts 1:8, Gal.6:10 NIV, Heb.12:2, John 3:16, Heb.13:5, Phil.4:13, Ps.37:23-24, Is.41:10 AMP, John 6:63, Matt.7:14, 1John 2:16, EZK.22:30

72. Ex.8:16, John2:7-11,1Cor.12:7-11, 1Cor.12:31, John 6:5-14, Acts 5:1-10, Acts 6:8;15:12;19:11

73. Ecc.3:1-3, Job 14:14, Ecc.3:1-2;7-8, Phil.4:11-12, Heb.9:27, Dan.2:21, Heb.13:8, Ps.139:14, Rev.1:8, Matt.24:35, Rom.8:28, 1Cor.3:6, Acts 9:1-6;20-21, Gen.1:11;27-30, Heb.1:3

74. Ps.91:3-5 EXB, Rom.8:28, Ps.40:2, 1Pet.5:7, Phil.4:6-7, Is.55:9, Ex.14:13 EXB, Is.41:10

75. Rom.9:4 AMP, Is.40:28 AMP, Ezk.24:14 AMP, Heb.13:5 AMP, Phil.4:19, Eph.1:5 AMP, Jer.29:11, Rom.8:30, Mark 12:30, Ex.20:3;5, John 3:16, Is.41:10, Num.21:3, John 17:17, Heb.4:16, Ps.37:5-8 EXB, Heb.11:6, Heb.10:23

76. Eph.2:10 AMP, John 1:12, 2Pet.1:3, 2Tim.3:16-17, 2Cor.5:18, John 14:26, 2Pet.1:3, Rom.5:1-5 AMP, Rom.8:28, Pro.3:5-6, Rom.8:35-39

Printed in the United States
By Bookmasters